PASSPORT TO SUCCESS

by Jessica Chen / Mark A. Pengra

LEARNING PUBLISHING CO., LTD.

編者的話

——您是個朝九晚五的上班族嗎？您是否想過該為自己的上班生涯，多開拓一片新天地呢？

做個高附加值的上班族

無論您是身為經理級的決策人員，還是力求表現的基層業務人員，一口流利的**英語**都是您日後獲得升遷的資產。本公司有鑑於此，特別針對上班族的實際需要，精心編成本書。只要您讀完本書，就能在短時間內掌握**商用英語**的精華，克服英語「**短路**」的煩惱，使您在工作上得心應手，更上一層樓。

迅速充電掌握未來

本書共分九章，收羅了上班族必備的**專業知識**和一般**常識**。以下分別介紹本書菁華部分：

◇ **企業英語熱身派**：本章包涵了上班族實用的基礎英語，如基本書信寫法，撥通國際電話等。另外亦附有上班前的準備運動，讓您從容就赴職業競技場，大展身手。

◇ **英語大談生意經**：從約會的安排、商務洽談、定契約到社交應酬，提供您一套完整的英語會話策略。

◇ **商務文件面面觀**：透過生動的對話，讓您了解重要商務文件，如信用狀、裝船文件的功能。

◇ **琳瑯滿目話商展**：本章教您熟悉從策劃參展到佈置、展示商品的實用語句。

◇ **爲個人和公司設計形象**：在注重包裝的工商社會，第一印象往往是日後生意成敗的關鍵。本章教您如何向客戶自我介紹，為個人及公司建立形象。

◇ **電話熱線的魅力**：電話早已是辦公室中的寵兒，本章教您如何應對接聽，與客戶來電 。

◇ **出差充電專輯**：出差是上班族另一出擊的戰場。本章讓您迅速充電，儲備實力，順利達成任務。

本書不僅是您開拓職業生涯不可缺少的**伙伴**，更是您案頭必備的實用手册。

本公司任何一本書的完成，皆經過審慎的編輯及多次的校閱，本書也不例外。但恐尚有疏漏之處，祈各界先進不吝指正。

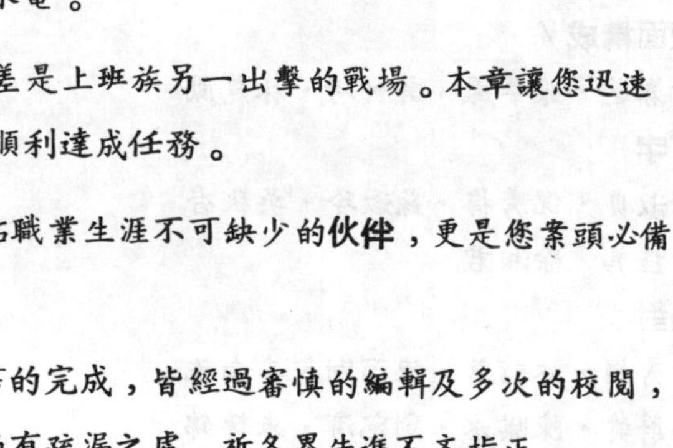

CONTENTS

Chapter 1 企業英語熱身派 1

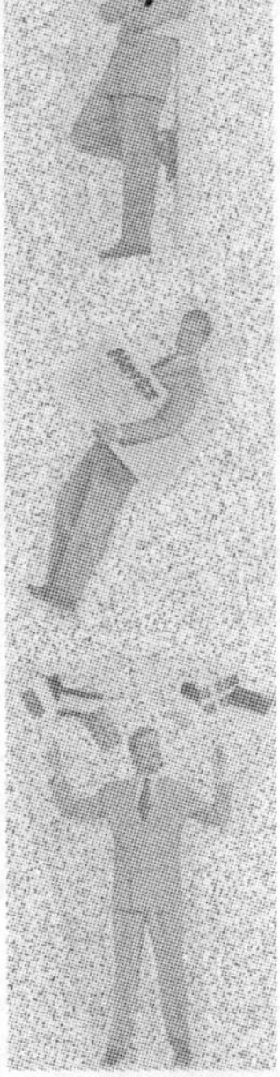

Chapter 2 英語大談生意經 41

Chapter 3 商務文件面面觀

Chapter 4 琳琅滿目話商展

Chapter 5 爲個人和公司設計形象

Chapter 6 電話熱線的魅力

Chapter 7 出差充電專輯

Chapter 8 辦公室花絮 239

Chapter 9 充電實用資訊篇 264

本書採用米色宏康護眼印書紙，版面清晰自然，
不傷眼睛。

CHAPTER 1

企業英語熱身派

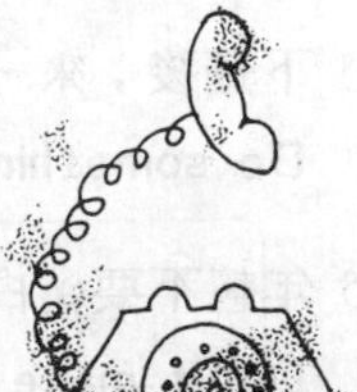

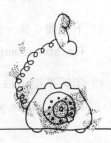

Part 1

工商人每日一句

Modern Talks

《 office hour 》

你知道現在流行說些什麼嗎？每日一句，讓你的英語會話，也充滿了流行的魅力，突出你的個性，爲上班生活加把勁！

A：I'm so tired of routine work. 我對例行的工作感到厭倦。

B：Why don't you take a vacation? ***To rest is to take longer walks.***
你爲什麼不休假一陣子呢？休息是爲了走更長遠的路。

A：You are right! I should ***add a little originality into my life.*** 你說得對！我應該爲生活加點創意。

我知道我的未來不是夢。
I know that my future is not just a dream.

休息是爲了走更長遠的路。
To rest is to take longer walks.

爲生活加點創意。
Add a little originality into your life.

下班後，來一點別的吧！
Do something different after work hours!

年輕不要留白。
Don't make your younger days a blank sheet.

ღ 反敗爲勝。

To convert defeat into victory.

ღ 1988 龍行奧運。

1988 is both the year of the dragon (Chinese) and the Olympics.

ღ 這是一個注重自我包裝的時代。

This is an age where self-packaging is important.

ღ 做個高附加值的上班族。

Be a salaried worker of high added value.

ღ 大家一起來。

Everybody come together.（此句爲命令句，故不用 comes，而用 come。）

ღ 我受夠了！

I can't bear it any longer！

ღ 年輕就是無限的可能。

Youth means limitless possibilities.

ღ 給你一個良心的建議。

I'll give you conscientious advice.

ღ 人怕出名，豬怕肥。

People are afraid to be famous.（like the pig is afraid to get fat.）

ღ 留給下一代一個乾淨的地球。

Leave behind a clean world for future generations.

ღ 做人要甘願一點！

Upright people are always willing to help others.

ʊ 妻子是永遠的情人。

Your wife is your eternal lover.

ʊ 禮輕情意重。

Though the gift is small, the feeling is great.

ʊ 你也做得到！

You can do it too!

ʊ 心事誰人知？

Who knows my heart?

ʊ 跟著感覺走。

Let your feelings lead you.

ʊ 隨時給自己鼓勵一下。

Encourage yourself once in a while.

ʊ 珍惜每一次相遇！

Cherish each encounter!

ʊ 沒有人是十全十美的。

No one is perfect.

ʊ 開創職業生涯的另一高峯。

Get to another summit in your career.

ʊ 追求自我的突破。

Pursue breakthroughs in your life.

ʊ 誰說愛情是盲目的？

Who says love is blind?

Part 2

上班前的準備運動

Warming Up Before Work

● **狀況**：明天突然要去參加商業午餐。

困難：雖想積極展開交談，無奈沒有聊天的話題。

方法與對策 ⇨ 看當地的新聞，瞭解當地的生活情況。

實踐範例 ⇨

◇ Is there anything new？有什麼新鮮的事嗎？

◇ The " New York Times " this morning says......

今早的紐約時報報導......

● **狀況**：在會議中，必須發表有關新產品的介紹演說。

困難：雖然事先擬了草稿，但在會議進行中，沒有把握能講得和草稿一樣流暢。

方法與對策 ⇨ 把資料的要點，前後連貫地寫在紙上。每個項目要有系統，條理分明，別人比較聽得懂。

實踐範例 ⇨

◇ Let me begin with...... 讓我以......開始。

◇ *I have three major points to discuss with you.*

我有三個重點要和你們討論。

◇ Are there any questions？有任何問題嗎？

◇ Thank you very much (for your attention).

非常謝謝你們（的參加）。

● **狀況**：到中正機場去迎接客戶。

困難：由於是第一次見面，不知道開始要說些什麼話。

方法與對策 ⇨ 深呼吸一下，然後以簡易的寒喧會話和對方打招呼。記得面帶微笑。

實踐範例 ⇨

◇ Hello, Mr. C！ 嗨，C先生！

◇ I suspect you're tired after a long flight.
　我想經過長途飛行，你應該累了吧。

◇ Did you have a comfortable flight？你的航程還舒服嗎？

● **狀況**：明天是第一天上班的日子。

困難：不知道要如何穿著裝備才好。

方法與對策 ⇨ 上班時間的穿著，要力求方便工作與舒適爲主。一般職業婦女，會選擇連身套裝或窄裙，鞋子則以平底或稍帶跟的便鞋，切記不要濃粧艷抹，珠光寶氣。若使用香水，也以古龍水等較清淡的香味爲主。頭髮爲便於整理起見，也不宜太長。致於男性，則以西裝爲主，較不正式的場合，亦可穿著輕便的休閒服飾，但切記勿穿著牛仔褲、布鞋。

實踐範例 ⇨

● **狀況**：被招待參加雞尾酒會。

困難：不知是否能與客戶打成一片，暢談生意以外的話題。

方法與對策 ⇨ 宴會是收集情報，和擴大交際的重要場合。要從準備自己專精的話題或笑話著手。

實踐範例 ⇨

◇ I've been loaded down with many things these days, such as…
這幾天我有很多事情要忙，比如……

◇ Tell me about your family. 告訴我有關你家裡的事。

◇ Can I join you？我可以參加嗎？

● **狀況**：辦公桌上文件堆積如山，文具用品零亂不堪。

困難：要找的檔案文件遍尋不著。

方法與對策 ⇨ 將桌面上的文具用品固定位置，memo 放在電話旁邊，即期的文件置於案前，過期的檔案，則歸入檔案櫃。每一件case都用文件夾歸類好。抽屜中的物品，可列一張明細表壓在桌面玻璃下，方便找尋。常用的電話號碼、地址也可壓在玻璃下。桌面儘量少放東西，保持足夠的工作空間。

實踐範例 ⇨

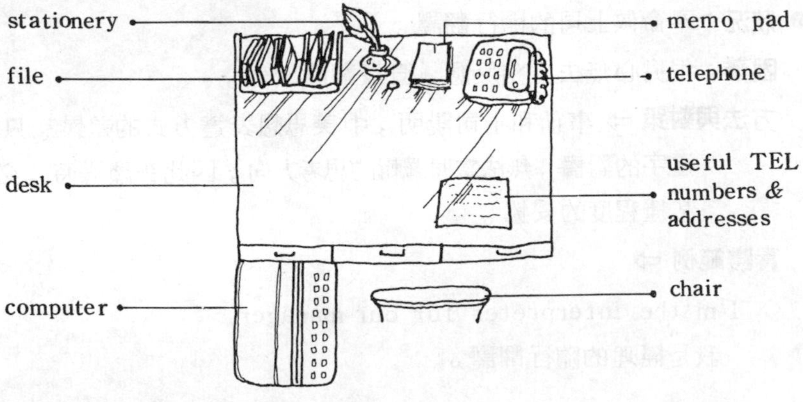

● **狀況**：好幾年沒到美國出差了，最近就要去了。

困難：太久沒講英語，無法跟上美國人講話的速度。

方法與對策 ⇨ 一方面收聽英語廣播，加強速聽練習。一方面購買商用會話之類的書籍，惡補一番。當然平常就儲備實力，以備不時之需，是最好不過了。

實踐範例 ⇨ ICRT — International Community Radio Taiwan, 空中英語教室、今日美語等廣播節目。

● **狀況**：有一大堆的英文資料。下星期會議中，一定要做出報告。

困難：有能力譯讀或精讀，但沒那麼多時間。

方法與對策 ⇨ 找出文章中的標題，並將要點劃線。一個段落有一個 *topic sentence*，爲重要的關鍵。開頭的 *introduction* 部分也很重要。

實踐範例 ⇨ 妨礙英文理解度的主要原因：

1. 對外界反應的速度和正確性
2. 記憶力
3. 動機
4. 預想能力
5. 語彙能力
6. 集中力
7. 知識或經驗的背景
8. 批判性的讀書能力。

● **狀況**：奉命做上司的隨行翻譯。

困難：很擔心無法立刻反應，直接翻譯出來。

方法與對策 ⇨ 事前和上司說明，中美思想表達方式的差異。只透過逐字的對譯，無法掌握邏輯的思考方向，因此在翻譯時，必須做某種程度的妥協。

實踐範例 ⇨

◇ I'm the interpreter for our manager.

我是經理的隨行翻譯。

◇ We want to know.... 我們想知道…。

◇ He means that.... 他的意思是…。

◇ Yes, unless the market price fluctuates.
是的，除非市場價格波動。

◇ No, as long as S + V ...... 不，只要主詞＋動詞……

◇ Yes, when...... No, when ～. 是的，當……時。不，當…時。

● **狀況**：被命令以二星期的期限，做出美國的市場調查。

困難：要如何從自誇頑強的外國客戶手中，套出眞心話。

方法與對策 ⇨ 用"*why*"來展開攻勢。與對方站在平等互惠的立場，也給予客戶一些情報。談話時，眼睛正視對方，避免詢問個人隱私。

實踐範例 ⇨

◇ Let me ask you, point-blank, about....
讓我坦白地問你有關……

◇ What's the reason for the sales drop?
業績下降的原因是什麼？

◇ Let me get it straight. 讓我坦白說吧。

● **狀況**：與對酒食非常有心得的Y先生會面。

困難：不談生意經，專談些品酒的內容，沒有辦法隨聲附和。

方法與對策 ⇨ 趕快讀幾本有關於酒的書藉，或查百科全書，收集一些可充當話題，有關酒的名稱、產地等的情報。

實踐範例 ⇨

◇ Tell me what's the appeal of wine.
告訴我酒的魅力何在。

◇ Why did you get into wine? 你爲什麼開始喝酒？

◇ How does American wine compare with French wine？
美國酒和法國酒，比起來怎樣？

● **狀況**：公司要爲自己的產品，做英文廣告的文案草稿 。

困難：卽使能寫出文法正確的英語，但萬一被認爲沒有吸引力的話…

方法與對策 ⇨ 明確地指出與其他公司不同的優點。文案要簡短有力，可參考國外的廣告文案，構思創意。注意不要寫出 *Chinese English*，必要時可請老外參與 。

實踐範例 ⇨ 英語書寫的要訣：

1. Be clear ／清晰
2. Be complete ／完整
3. Be concise ／簡明
4. Be correct ／正確
5. Be creative ／創造性
6. Be considerate ／貼切

Part 3

基本商業書信

Basic Business Letters

書寫商業往來信件，是從事國際貿易者的必備能力之一。要寫出一封形式內容皆宜的商業書信，必須注意以下各點：

※ 1. 下筆之前，要先考慮收信的**對象**。如果是第一次做生意的客戶，就必須採取較**正式**的語法與形式，因此要避免使用**俚語**之類的詞句，注意禮貌的周到。若是寫給較熟悉的客戶，則可採用**較平易近人**的稱呼及用字。

※ 2. 書信的內容要力求**簡單明瞭**。在繁忙的商場中，冗長或語意不清的詞句，會令人失去耐心。最好一個段落，只陳述一個主題，多使用**肯定**及**主動**的語氣，避免過度使用逗點和關係代名詞。

※ 3. 平常就應該多**練習**書信的寫作。熟記一些**實用**的句型，一般而言，商業書信都有一定的格式可循，只要多看多寫，即可寫出一手漂亮的英文書信。

基本書信範例

<❶開發信 A>

Gentlemen:

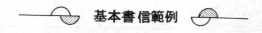

Your firm has been introduced to us by Messrs. ABC & Co., Wisconsin, U.S.A. So we are writing to you to ask if you feel disposed to do direct business with us.

For over 70 years, we have been one of the biggest manufacturers of Gold and Silver Threads in Taiwan, ***enjoying a good reputation*** as a regular supplier to the leading factories and dealers here.

According to the suggestion of the firm mentioned above, we are enclosing our samples for your inspection.

These threads are supplied on 10-yard skeins in both gold and silver. The present price is $1.60 each per skein, CIF your port. ***For a large quantity order some discount will be allowed.***

We do hope that you may find this offer sufficiently attractive to give us your initial order soon.

Very truly yours,

敬啓者：

美國威斯康辛的ABC公司，曾向本公司引薦貴公司，因此我們寫信詢問貴公司，是否願意和我們直接貿易。

七十年以來，我們一直是台灣金銀金屬細線的最大製造廠商，並且是此地主要工廠和貿易商，信譽絕佳的供貨者。

基於上述公司的建議，我們附上本公司的樣本，供您檢示。

這些樣本是以十碼為一束的金銀細線。目前的價格是一束1.6美元，包括到港口的運費和保險費在內。如果您大批訂購，將享有特惠的折扣。

我們希望這次的報價，會引起貴公司的興趣，而能夠儘快下訂單給我們。

敬祝愉快

＊Notes

Messrs.〔ˈmɛsɚz〕*n.pl*. Messieurs 的縮形（用作*Mr*. 的複數形）
thread〔θrɛd〕*n*. 線；纖維　　skein〔sken〕*n*. 一束

＜❷開發信 B＞

Gentlemen：

We have learned from "World Trade News", a weekly magazine issued by the Institute for International Commerce in Taipei, that you are one of the leading importers of Cameras in your country. We, therefore, take pleasure in informing you that we have recently completed the production of a new model entitled "PANEX" whose high efficiency has been proven by ***a scrupulous test of its mechanism and functions as clearly explained in our illustrated catalog inclosed.***

We believe that considering the improvements it offers, you will find our PANEX a very good seller at the competitive price of US$110.00 CIF San Francisco including the cost of accessories. Like all other cameras we handle, PANEX is also accompanied with a ***two-year guarantee as our after-sale service.***

If you have interest in dealing with us in PANEX or other types of cameras shown in our catalog, please inform us of your requirements as well as your bankers' name and address.

We assure you of our best service.

Yours very truly,

敬啓者：

我們從台北的國際通商機構，所出版的「世界貿易週刋」上，得知貴公司爲貴國的主要相機進口商之一。因此，我們很榮幸能告知您，我們最近剛開發完成一種新機型「拍耐克斯」，它的高效率，已被機械裝置和功能的嚴謹測試所證明。在附寄的目錄中，我們備有清楚的說明。

我們相信，在考慮過這些優點之後，貴公司將會發現「拍耐克斯」將會非常暢銷。我們的報價是美金110元，包括到舊金山的運費、保險費和附件的價格在內。和我們其它相機一樣，「拍耐克斯」享有兩年的品質保證和售後服務。

如果貴公司對「拍耐克斯」或目錄上其它機型感興趣的話，請通知我們貴公司的交易條件、銀行和地址。

我們保證提供您最佳的服務。

敬祝愉快

*** Notes**

scrupulous〔'skrupjələs〕*adj.* 嚴謹的　mechanism〔'mɛkə,nɪzm̩〕*n.* 機械裝置
inclose〔ɪn'kloz〕*v.* 隨信附上　accessory〔æk'sɛsərɪ〕*n.* 附件

<❸請求報價A>

Gentlemen:

Will you please quote us your best prices on stainless steel tableware, i. e., knives, forks, spoons. Your prices should be based on 5000 gross pieces. ***Prices are preferred on a CIF basis***. The delivery time will also be an important factor.

Samples, illustrative matter, and all pertinent data you may furnish us will be helpful and greatly appreciated. The contents and composition of the metal will determine what our import duty will be.

Your immediate cooperation is urgently needed.

Yours truly,

敬啓者：

能否請貴公司爲不銹鋼餐具，例如餐刀、叉子、湯匙，報上最便宜的價格？請以五千件爲一組報價，最好包括運費和保險費在內。交貨的日期也是個重要因素。

如果貴公司能提供樣本、說明書、和其它相關的資料給我們，那將會有所助益，我們也會非常感激。容量和金屬的構造，將會影響我們的進口關稅額。

我們急需貴公司的立即協助。

*** Notes**

quote〔kwot〕*v*. 報價　　***stainless steel*** 不銹鋼
pertinent〔'pɜtənənt〕*adj*. 相關的；有關的
furnish〔'fɜnɪʃ〕*v*. 提供；供給　　contents〔kən'tɛnts〕*n.pl*. 容量

＜❹請求報價B＞

Gentlemen:

Your name and address have been given to us by the Taipei Chamber of Commerce and Industry as a large exporter of cosmetics. We are specially interested in importing lipsticks and face powders.

If you can assure us of workable prices, excellent quality, and prompt delivery, we shall be able to deal in these goods on a substantial scale. We, therefore, request you to furnish us with ***a full range of*** samples, assorted colors together with your lowest quotations and other terms and conditions.

As to our ***credit standing***, please refer to the following bank:

The Bank of Taiwan, Keelung Branch
(address)
....

Your immediate reply would be highly appreciated.

Yours very truly,

敬啓者:

台北工商協會告知我們，貴公司是化粧品的大型外銷廠商，並提供我們貴公司的名稱和地址。我們對唇膏和蜜粉的進口特別有興趣。

如果貴公司可以保證有利的價格、絕佳的品質和立即交貨，我們將大量地訂購這些貨品。因此，我們要求貴公司提供完整的樣品、種類顏色、最低的報價和其它交易條件。

至於我們的信用問題，請諮詢下列銀行：

台灣銀行，基隆分行

（地址）

……………………………………………………………

我們期望貴公司儘快回信。

敬祝愉快

* **Notes**

substantial〔 səb'stænʃəl 〕*adj*. 大量的　　***credit standing*** 信用

＜❺ 要求樣本＞

Gentlemen:

Thank you for the TAISHO Battery list.

We chose three items and will appreciate your sending us one sample each of:

1. No. 222　Midget ball point pen light
2. No. 333　Pencil light
3. No. 444　Fountain pen flashlight

Please airmail us all three samples, if possible, with prices.

A check for $5.00 is enclosed. If not sufficient, please let us know. ***We will remit the balance***.

Thank you.　　　　Very truly yours,

敬啓者：

感謝貴公司寄來的「泰壽」電池名單。

我們選擇了三種產品，希望貴公司能爲我們寄上每一種產品的樣品。我們將非常感激。

1. No. 222 迷你原子筆照明燈
2. No. 333 鉛筆照明燈
3. No. 444 自來水筆手電筒

如果可能的話，請航空郵寄三種樣品及其價格。

信中附上美金5元。如果還不夠，請告知我們。我們將滙寄補上餘額。

謝謝您！

敬祝安好

＊ Notes

battery 〔ˈbætərɪ〕 ***n.*** 電池　**midget** 〔ˈmɪdʒɪt〕 ***adj.*** 迷你的
remit 〔rɪˈmɪt〕 ***v.*** 滙寄　**balance** 〔ˈbæləns〕 ***n.*** 餘額

<❻收到樣品>

Gentlemen：

We received your sample with thanks. If you can accept $2.75 per set F.O.B. Kobe, send us a proforma invoice and we shall be ready to book 1,000 sets of WW-567. ***A letter of credit will be established immediately.*** When shipping the merchandise we need your assurance that the quality will be as high as that of the sample.

Yours truly,

敬啓者：

我們已經收到貴公司寄來的樣品。如果貴公司能接受每組起岸價格 2.75 美元，請寄給我們一份預約形式發票，我們將訂購一千組 WW-567 型的產品。信用狀將會立即開出。當貨物裝船時，我們需要貴公司保證，貨物的品質和樣品一致。

敬祝安好

*** Notes**

proforma〔proʹfɔrmə〕*adj*. 形式上的　invoice〔ʹɪnvɔɪs〕*n*. 發票
letter of credit 信用狀　merchandise〔ʹmɜtʃən,daɪz〕*n*. 貨物；商品

<❻回答報價>

Gentlemen:

With many thanks for your inquiry of July 15, 19××, we are very glad to send you separately the samples of lipsticks and face powders together with the respective price-lists.

Please note that Item No. L-115 and No. FP-25 can be certainly promised for immediate shipment upon receipt of your order, subject to the establishment of ***an Irrevocable and Confirmed Letter of Credit*** for the corresponding amount of order, valid for a period of 60 days.

We wish to invite your special attention to the fact that the increasing cost of raw materials for these articles will compel us to raise their selling prices, and that the present prices can no longer be guaranteed.

We trust that your initial order will be placed with us without delay.

Yours very truly,

敬啓者：

非常感謝貴公司七月十五日的詢問信，我們非常高興，能爲您分別寄上唇膏和蜜粉的樣品和個別的價目表。

請注意，No. L-115 和No. FP-25 可以在收到訂單後，立即送貨，但必須依照訂單上的金額，開立不可撤銷信用狀，有效期限爲六十天。

我們希望您能了解，這些產品的原料價格上漲，將會迫使我們調高售價，而且目前的價格將無法保證持續太久。

我們確信，將會很快收到您的訂單。

敬祝安好

*** Notes**

subject〔'sʌbdʒɪkt〕*adv*. 須以…爲條件；倘若；遵照
valid〔'vælɪd〕*adj*. 依法有效的　**compel**〔kəm'pɛl〕*v*. 強迫
guarantee〔,gærən'ti〕*v*. 保證

＜❽抱怨信件＞

Dear Sirs,

Our customers ***are very annoyed about*** this particular design: black is the most important color and it is next to impossible to sell the other shades without black.

Steve also pointed out that separate shipment of the black item will cost an extra freight and extra clearing charges at this end.

Nor is this all. Our clients claim that the shade shown in the shipping sample is not exactly what was ordered and that it is not acceptable for men's shirts.

We fear that a very stiff claim will be made on the third point and suggest that you should contact the weavers and send us an offer of what you are prepared to pay to settle this point.

Please give us your comments by return post.

Yours faithfully,

敬啓者：

我們的顧客對這種特殊的設計，非常不滿：黑色是最主要的顏色，要賣不包括黑色的其它色調產品，幾乎是不可能。

史蒂夫公司也指出，這些黑色產品的分開裝船，導致他們，最後必須付額外的運費和票據交換費。

還不只這些。我們的客戶抱怨裝船樣品的色調，和所訂購產品的色調不同，而且男士襯衫，無法使用這些產品。

我們恐怕必須對第三點提出強硬的聲明，並且建議貴公司和織工聯繫之後，儘速通知我們，貴公司準備如何解決這件事。

請回函時，告知我們您的意見爲何。

*** Notes**

annoy〔ə'nɔɪ〕*v*. 使煩惱　shade〔ʃed〕*n*. 色調
weaver〔'wivɚ〕*n*. 織工　stiff〔stɪf〕*adj*. 強硬的

<⑨回覆抱怨信件A>

Dear Sirs,

We acknowledge receipt of your letter No. E213.

We do not consider that the responsibility lies fully with us. The wrong colorings are due originally to the absence of particular notes in your instructions.

Our weavers have done a fine job as far as the color matching is concerned though ***in view of*** the result they may have been too faithful to the instructions.

It seems very severe, then, that you ***set down*** the wrong coloring wholly to us. In fact, we are unable to ask our weavers to meet the claim, and so suggest that ***you leave the matter until the time of our next transaction*** on Fancy Cotton with this firm, when we shall be sure to meet part of their loss.

Yours faithfully,

敬啓者：

茲收到貴公司編號E213號的來信。

我們並不認爲，必須負全部的責任。錯誤的配色，主要是歸咎於貴公司最初並沒有特別的指示。

我們的織工就配色方面而言，一向非常盡職，即使是鑑於結果，可能會太過於遵照指示。

然而，貴公司將配色錯誤的所有責任歸於我們，似乎有失厚道。

事實上，我們無法要求織工接受這項聲明，並且建議貴公司，將這件事情留待下次和這家工廠交易上等棉布時再討論，到時，我們確信能補償他們的部分損失。

敬祝安好

*** Notes**

originally〔ə'rɪdʒənəlɪ〕*adv*. 最初　　***as far as*** ～ 就～而言
severe〔sə'vɪr〕*adj*. 嚴厲的；苛刻的　　transaction〔træn'zækʃən〕*n*.交易

＜⑩回覆抱怨信件B＞

Dear Sirs,

We acknowledge receipt of your letter No. E267.

We are giving our attention to the matter and will give you a reply probably by next week.

Yours faithfully,

敬啓者：

茲收到貴公司編號E267號的來信。

我們正全力處理此事，並且約在下星期給您答覆。

敬祝安好

*** Notes**

acknowledge〔ək'nɑlɪdʒ〕*v*. 承認收到（信件等）

<❶請帖A>

Mr. & Mrs. John Wang

Request the pleasure of your company at dinner on Sunday Sept. 4, 1988 at 7 o'clock P.M.

Address : AMBASSADOR HOTEL, VIP ROOM, 63 Chung Shan N. Road, Sec. 2

Phone No : 5511111

R.S.V.P.

謹訂於一九××年九月四日（星期日）下午七時晚宴，屆時敬請光臨

王約翰夫婦　謹訂

地址：國賓飯店，名人廳，中山北路二段63號
電話：5511111
候覆：

<❷請帖B>

Mr. and Mrs. John Wang

Request the pleasure of your company for dinner at home on September fourth from six o'clock to eight P.M.

Address : 3 , Alley 8. Lane 348, Minchuan E. Road,
Taipei, R.O.C.
Phone No : 7510432
R.S.V.P.

謹訂於九月四日下午六時至八時舉行晚宴，屆時敬請光臨

王約翰夫婦　謹訂

地址：台北市民權東路 348 巷 8 弄 3 號
電話：7510432
候覆：

＜❷**覆信A**＞

Sept. 2 , 19××

Dear Mr. & Mrs. John Wang,

We are happy to accept your invitation for dinner on Sept. 4.

Sincerely,

Peter Chen

承蒙　閣下夫婦惠邀於九月四日晚宴，屆時定當準時前往。

此致

王約翰夫婦

陳彼得　敬覆

一九××年九月二日

<❸覆信B>

Sept. 2, 19××.

Dear Mr. Wang

I am sorry but we cannot attend the dinner you are holding on Sept. 4. We have a previous engagement that is preventing our coming, but ***thank you for the invitation.***

Sincerely,

Peter Chen

王先生：

承蒙　閣下夫婦惠邀於本月四日晚宴，因事先有約，不克前來參加，甚歉；並致謝忱。

陳彼得　敬覆

一九××年九月二日

● Hint Bank —折疊信紙迷你情報

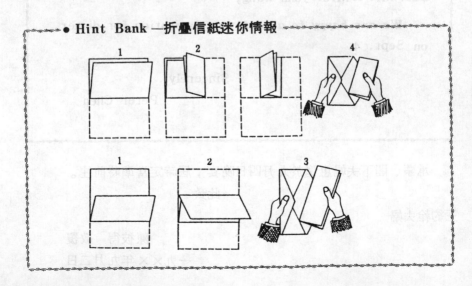

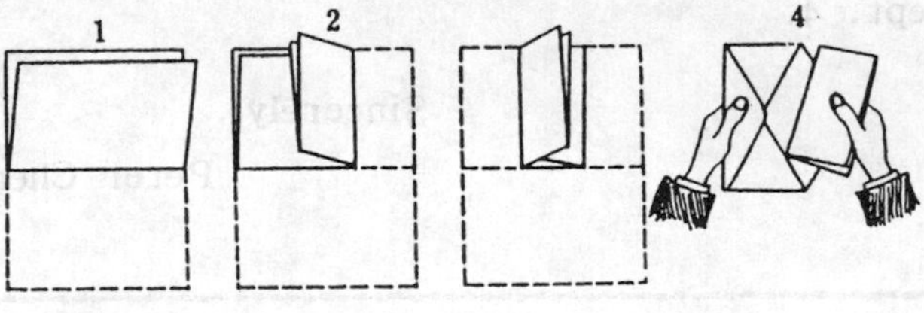

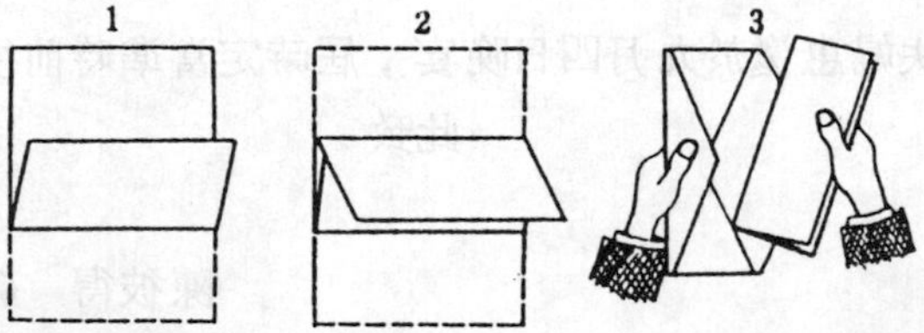

Part 4

如何撥通國際電話

How to Place an International Call

商業溝通講求**速度**。如果說，現在的辦公室，正是國際電話的天下，是一點也不爲過。特別是當你配屬在國外部或國際部門時，首先令你頭痛的，應該是如何應付國際電話。本節正是爲「被國際電話搞得**神經衰弱**」的你而整理的。如果你認爲「國際電話是最溫柔的工作伙伴」。那麼也請你再次複習，好嗎？

國際電話的種類

(1) **國際直撥電話**（ *International Subscriber Dialing* ）

不透過國際電話局的接線生，直接撥通對方國家的國際電話。現在爲美國、歐洲、韓國、台灣等國家所廣泛應用。

撥號順序：國際冠碼（ *INT'L PREFIX* ）＋國碼（ *COUNTRY CODE* ）＋區域號碼（ *AREA CODE* ）＋用戶電話號碼（ *CALLED LOCAL NO.* ）

(2) **國際叫號電話**（ *Station Call* ）

也稱爲 *Station-to-Station Call*，指定對方電話號碼的國際電話，經常被使用。

(3) **指名電話**（ *Personal Call* ）

也稱爲 *Person-to-Person Call* ，指定對方本人接聽的電話，在對方沒來接電話之前，不計電話費。也可以指定「房間號碼」、「部門名稱」等，不一定要指定人名。不過這類電話的費用相當高。

(4) **對方付費電話**(***Collect Call***)

請受話人付費的電話。接線生會先徵求受話人的同意，才通話。通話完畢後，可請接線生報出時間和費用。在海外，想打電話報平安時，可利用此種電話。

(5) **信用卡電話**(***Credit Card Call***)

到電信局申請一張信用卡(***credit card***)，可以在打過電話後，再由信用卡契約上，所指定的公司或個人支付。非常方便。不過如果信用卡不慎遺失，則有被人冒用的危險。

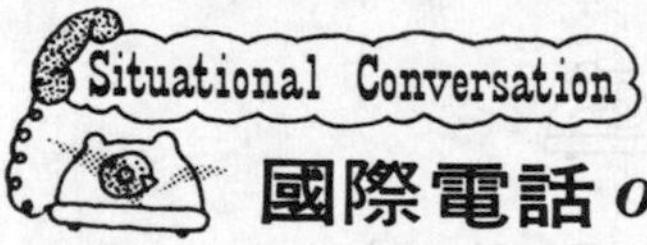

國際電話 *Overseas Telephone Call*

接線生： Is this the Silver Star Trading Company?
這裡是銀星貿易公司嗎？

中國人： Yes, it is. 是的。

接線生： This is the overseas telephone operator in the United States. ***We have a call for*** Mr. John Wang in the International Finance Department from a Mr. Robert of ABC Company in New York.
我是美國的國際電話接線生。紐約 ABC 公司的羅伯先生，要請你們國際財務部的王約翰先生聽電話。

中國人： From whom, did you say? 你說是誰打來的？

接線生： From a Mr. Robert of ABC Company in New York.
紐約ABC公司的羅伯先生。

中國人： Thank you. ***Just hold the line, please.***
謝謝。請稍等一會兒。

～幾秒鐘後～

中國人： Hello. I'm sorry but Mr. John Wang is in a conference right now. 喂。很抱歉，王約翰先生正在開會。

接線生： Oh, is that right? When will he be free?
噢，眞的嗎？他什麼時候會在呢？

中國人： Well, he'll be free around four o'clock.
嗯，他大概四點左右會在。

接線生： I see. Just a minute, please.
我知道了。請稍候一會。

～幾秒鐘後～

接線生： Hello. ***How about*** Mr. Peter Chen, then?
喂，那麼，陳彼得先生在嗎？

中國人： Yes, he's here. One moment, please.
是的，他在。請等一下。

～暫停～

**

operator〔'ɑpə,retɚ〕*n.* 接線生　　conference〔'kɑnfərəns〕*n.* 會議

陳彼得： Hello. ***This is Peter Chen speaking.***
喂。我是陳彼得。

接線生： Oh, Mr. Chen？***Will you hold the line, please***？
噢，陳先生嗎？請等一下好嗎？

～暫停～

接線生： ***Thank you for waiting***. Mr. Robert is on the line. Go ahead, please. 久等了。已接通羅伯先生了。請通話。

陳彼得： Thank you. 謝謝你。

國際電話 *Overseas Telephone Call*

♧ ... Hello. May I speak to Mr. Brown？
喂。我可以和伯朗先生說話嗎？

♧ ***Yes, this is he speaking***. 我就是。

♧ ***Who's speaking, please***？請問您是哪位？

♧ I'm sorry, he is not in now. 很抱歉，他現在不在。

♧ ***Would you like to leave a message***？您要留話嗎？

♧ Mr. Brown is ***on another line now***. 伯朗先生的電話佔線中。

♧ Hold the line a moment, please. 請稍等一會兒。

♧ May I have Ext. 6326？請幫我接內線6326好嗎？

♧ I can't hear you. 我聽不見你的聲音。

♧ ***Would you speak a little louder***？你可以大聲一點嗎？

♧ I'm sorry, I have the wrong number. 對不起，我打錯了。

♧ ***You are wanted*** on the phone. 你的電話。

♧ Will you ask him to ***call*** me ***back*** later？
你可以告訴他，稍候回電話給我嗎？

♧ ***I was cut off***. Will you connect me again？
我的通話被切斷了。請再爲我接通好嗎？

♧ We'll call you back in a few minutes. Will you ***hang up*** and wait, please？
幾分鐘後，我們再打給您。請先掛斷，稍等一會好嗎？

♧ I want to ***place an overseas call*** to New York.
我要打一通到紐約的越洋電話。

♧ Could you tell me the time and charges after the call？
通話後，請告訴我時間和費用好嗎？

♧ Sorry, I can't wait. Please cancel the call.
對不起，我不能等。請將通話取消。

♧ This is the Singapore operator. Would you ***connect*** me ***with*** Mr. Lee in the International Department？我是新加坡接線生。
請幫我接國際部的李先生好嗎？

♧ This is the overseas operator in the United States. You have an overseas collect call from Mr. Smith in San Francisco. ***Will you accept the charges***？我是美國的越洋接線生。你們有一通舊金山，史密斯先生打來的電話。你們願意付費嗎？

Part 5 必備重要簡稱

科　技

APL	a programming language	程式語言
AC/DC	alternating/direct current	交流電／直流電
BASIC	beginner's all-purpose symbolic instruction code	初學者多功能符號指示密碼
BIT	binary digit	二進位數字
CAD	computer-aided design	電腦輔助設計
CAM	computer-aided manufacturing	電腦輔助製造
CD	compact disc	磁碟片
CATV	cable television	有線電視
CG	computer graphics	電腦繪圖
COM	computer output on microfilm	顯微膠片輸出
COBOL	common business-oriented language	通用商業語言
DAM	direct access method	直接出入法
DAD	digital audio disc	有聲數位磁片
DBS	direct broadcasting satellite	直接廣播衛星

DDP	distributed data processing	分散型資料處理
DNA	deoxyribonucleic acid	去氧核糖核酸
FORTRAN	formula translator	公式翻譯語言
HDTV	high-definition TV	高解像力電視
IC	integrated circuit	積體電路
IEA	International Energy Agency	國際能源機構
INS	information network system	資訊網系統
INTELSAT	International Telecommunications Satellite	國際通訊衛星
ISAM	indexed sequential access method	索引順序出入法
LED	light-emitting diode	發光二極體
LSI	large scale integration	大型積體電路
MIPS	million instructions per second	每秒可接受一百萬個指令
MODEM	modulator-demodulator	變換調幅器
NC	numerical control	數值控制
OA	office automation	辦公室自動化
OCR	optical character recognition	感光辨字
OMR	optical mark recognition	感光符號辨認
OS	operation system	操作系統
RAM	random access memory	隨機進出記憶體

RNA	ribonucleic acid	核糖核酸
ROM	read only memory	唯讀記憶器
SAM	sequential access method	循序出入法
SP	structured programming	結構化程式
VAN	value added network	付加值通訊網
VLSI	very large scale integrated circuit	超大型積體電路

政治經濟

ASE	American Stock Exchange	美國證券交易所
ASEAN	Association of South-East Asian Nations	東南亞國協
CIA	Central Intelligence Agency	中央情報局
COCOM	Coordinating Committee for Exports to Communist Nations	對共產國家輸出控制委員會
COMECON	Council for Mutual Economic Assistance	東歐經濟互援會議
CPI	consumer price index	消費者物價指數
DEA	Drug Enforcement Administration	毒品管制局
EC	European Community	歐洲共同體
EEC	European Economic Community	歐洲經濟共同體

EFTA	Economic Free Trade Association——歐洲自由貿易協會
EIB	European Investment Bank——歐洲投資銀行
EMA	Economic Monetary Agreement——歐洲金融協定
FAO	Food and Agriculture Organization——（聯合國）糧食農業組織
FBI	Federal Bureau of Investigation——聯邦調查局
FRB	Federal Reserve Bank——聯邦準備銀行
GATT	General Agreement on Tariffs and Trade——貿易關稅一般協定
ICPO	International Criminal Police Organization——國際刑事警察組織
ILO	International Labor Organization——國際勞工組織
IMF	International Monetary Fund——國際金融基金
IOC	International Olympic Committee——國際奧林匹克委員會
NASA	National Aeronautics and Space Administration——美國太空總署
NNP	Net National Product——國民生產淨額
NATO	North Atlantic Treaty Organization——北大西洋公約組織
NICS	newly industrializing countries——新興工業國家

OECD Organization for Economic Cooperation and Development —— 經濟合作開發組織

OPEC Organization of Petroleum Exporting Countries —— 石油輸出國家組織

PLO Palestine Liberation Organization —— 巴勒斯坦解放組織

UNCTAD United Nations Conference on Trade and Development —— 聯合國貿易開發會議

UNESCO United Nations Educational, Scientific and Cultural Organization —— 聯合國教育科學文化組織

UNSC United Nations Security Council —— 聯合國安全理事會

UNICEF United Nations Children's Fund —— 聯合國兒童基金

貿易金融

AD automatic depositor —— 自動提款機

AIPPI International Association for Protection of Industrial Property —— 國際工業所有權保護協會

BA bank acceptance —— 銀行承兌票據

BIS Bank for International Settlement —— 國際裁決銀行

NTCD	negotiable time certificate of deposit ——	可轉讓定期儲金證明
CIF	cost, insurance and freight ——	包括保險、運費的價格
CMA	cash management account ——	現金管理帳戶
CPI	consumer price index ——	消費者物價指數
EPC	Economic Policy Committee ——	經濟政策委員會
FA	factory automation ——	工廠自動化
ECU	European Currency Unit ——	歐洲貨幣單位
EMS	European Monetary System ——	歐洲貨幣制度
FOB	free on board ——	起岸價格
IMS	integrated manufacturing system ——	整合製造系統
IQ	import quota system ——	進口配額制
LR	Lloyd's Register of Shipping ——	勞埃船舶登記簿
LC	letter of credit ——	信用狀
MTN	multilateral trade - negotiation ——	多邊貿易交涉
NTB	non-tariff trade barrier ——	非關稅貿易壁壘
NCD	negotiable certificate of deposit ——	可轉讓儲金證明

OEM original equipment manufacturing ——— 初級設備製造業

OMA orderly marketing agreement ——— 市場秩序協定

R & D research and development ——— 研究開發

SWIFT Society for Worldwide Interbank Financial Telecommunications ——— 國際銀行通訊協會

TRT Trademark Registration Treaty ——— 商標登記條約

軍 事

ABC warfare atomic, biological and chemical warfare ——— 核子，生化戰爭

ASAT anti-satellite weapon ——— 反衛星武器

BMD ballistic missile defense ——— 防衛彈道飛彈系統

CCV control configured vehicle ——— 完全控制飛行的飛機

ICBM intercontinental ballistic missile ——— 洲際彈道飛彈

INF intermediate nuclear force ——— 中距離核子武器

IRBM intermediate range ballistic missile ——— 中距離彈道飛彈

MIRV	multiple independently targeted reentry vehicle	多彈頭飛彈
SALT	the Strategic Arms Limitation Talks	戰略武器限制談判
SDI	Strategic Defense Initiative	主動戰略防衛
SDF	Self Defense Forces	（日本）自衛隊
START	the Strategic Arms Reduction Talks	削減戰略武器談判

時　間

GMT	Greenwich mean time	格林威治標準時
IDL	international date line	國際換日線
inst.	instant	這個月
prox.	proximo	下個月
ult.	ultimo	上個月

職　稱

MBA	Master of Business Administration	企管碩士
CPA	Certified Public Accountant	合格會計師
AD	art director	藝術指導
ABD	all but dissertation	博士課程
Ph.D	Doctor of Philosophy	大學博士
MA	Master of Arts	文學碩士

● 心得筆記欄 ●

CHAPTER 2

英語大談生意經

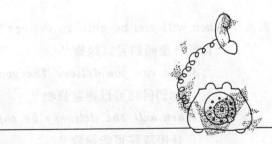

1. We'd like to order your products.

我們要訂購你們的產品。

● **One Point Advice**

接到**訂貨**(*order*)的電話，當然令人高興。但是如果不清楚是否有存貨時，該怎麼辦呢？這時你千萬不可先做主張，一定要先請買主稍等一下：***Will you wait while I see if we have them in stock?***（你能否等我看看我們是否有現貨？）否則不能如期交貨，反而會影響公司的**信譽**。

外國人：***We'd like to order your product, PCX.***

我們想訂購你們PCX型的產品。

⇨ *We've decided to order*... 我們決定訂購…

Do you have PCX in stock? 你們有PCX的現貨嗎？

中國人：I'll have that information by tomorrow.

我得明天才能知道消息。

⇨ *Will you wait while I see if we have them in stock?*

你能否等我看看我們是否有現貨？

I'm afraid our stock has run low. 恐怕我們的現貨不多。

外國人：When will you be able to deliver?

你們什麼時候可以送貨？

⇨ *When can you deliver the goods?*

你們何時可以運送貨物？

⇨ *When will the delivery be possible?*

什麼時候可能送貨？

中國人： Delivery takes at least one week after we have received your order.

至少要在我們收到你的訂單後一星期送貨。

➪ *We'll be able to deliver in three months.*

我們會在三個月內送貨。

➪ *The time of shipment will be around...*

裝運的時間大概在…

● Notes

order〔ˈɔrdɚ〕*v.* 訂購　　stock〔stɑk〕*n.* 存貨

information〔ˌɪnfɚˈmeʃən〕*n.* 消息　　deliver〔dɪˈlɪvɚ〕*v.* 遞送；送貨

shipment〔ˈʃɪpmənt〕*n.* 裝運；裝船

Hint Bank－貨運實用語彙

- ***trial order*** 試購訂單　　*air cargo* 空運貨物
- ***firm order*** 確定訂單　　indent〔ɪnˈdɛnt〕*n.* 代購訂單
- ***Ex ship*** 船上交貨　　*duty paid* 已納稅的
- ***cash on delivery*** 貨到付款　　***sold out*** 賣完

2. Your shipment hasn't arrived yet.

你們的船貨尚未到達。

● **One Point Advice**

當買主告知你貨物未如期到達時，***We are sorry for the delay***（我們爲延遲感到抱歉）是應對時最管用的一句話。除了耐心地解釋延遲的原因之外，並應允諾買主，這件事將迅速地被**處理**：***We'll deal with it as soon as possible***。

外國人：Your shipment hasn't arrived yet.

你們的船貨還沒到。

⇨ *There has been an excessive delay in shipment.*

裝運已躭擱太久了。

⇨ *The merchandise hasn't arrived yet.* 商品還沒到。

If it doesn't arrive by the tenth of June, we'll have to ***cancel the order***.

如果六月十日前還不到，我們就要取消訂單。

中國人：***We're sorry for the delay.*** The shipment has been delayed because of a port strike. ***We'll check into it*** and call you as soon as possible.

我們爲延遲感到抱歉，船貨躭擱是由於港口罷工。我們會仔細調查，並儘快通知你。

外國人：Furthermore, I received word that the merchandise has been damaged by water.

再者，我聽說貨物已被水損壞了。

In such a case, will full compensation be made?
果眞如此的話，會有完全賠償嗎？

中國人：Yes, we're fully insured. 是的，我們保了全險。

● Notes

delay〔dɪ'le〕*v*. 躭擱；延期　merchandise〔'mɝtʃən,daɪz〕*n*. 商品
strike〔straɪk〕*n*. 罷工　furthermore〔'fɝðɚ,mor,-,mɔr〕*adv*. 再者
damage〔'dæmɪdʒ〕*v*. 損壞　compensation〔,kɑmpən'seʃən〕*n*. 賠償
insure〔ɪn'ʃur〕*v*. 保險

Hint Bank－貨運實用語彙

- *gross weight* 總重；毛重　*repeat order* 再購訂單
- *carriage forward* 運費由收件人負擔
- *clean bill of exchange* 兌換證明書
- *insured amount* 保險金　*sea transportation* 海運
- *execution of order* 訂單的履行　*net weight* 淨重
- *a sight draft* 見票即付之支票或票據

3. The computer does not work properly.

電腦功能有問題。

● **One Point Advice**

一般公司對出售的產品都提供**售後服務**（***aftersale service***），尤其是較精密的儀器，如電腦，更是設有***systems engineer***（系統工程師）專門負責售後的維修工作（***maintenance***）。因此***We'll send a representative to check the cause.*** 是處理客戶**抱怨**時應熟記的句型。

顧　客：The computer we bought from you does not work properly. 我們向你買的電腦，運作不正常。

⇨ *Something is wrong with your product.*

你們的產品有些瑕疵。

⇨ *I'd like to complain about damaged goods.*

我對這些損壞的貨品非常不滿。

⇨ *The goods were damaged in transit.*

這些貨物在運送中被損壞了。

廠　商：I'm sorry to hear that. ***It's hard to believe.***

聽到這件事，我覺得很抱歉。眞難以置信。

What is the problem? 問題出在哪兒呢？

⇨ *What's wrong with your article?*

你的物件有什麼問題嗎？

We'll send a representative to check the cause. Please explain to him what the trouble is.

我們會派一位代表調查原因。請向他說明問題所在。

顧　客：All right, but there seems to be a problem with the packing. 好的，但是包裝上似乎有問題。

The packing seem to be too crude. 包裝似乎太草率了。

廠　商：***Is that so***？這樣子嗎？

Please accept our apologies for this problem.

請爲這項缺失，接受我們的道歉。

● Notes

complain〔kəm'plen〕*v*. 不滿；抱怨　　transit〔'trænsɪt, -zɪt〕*n*. 運送

representative〔,rɛprɪ'zɛntətɪv〕*n*. 代表　　packing〔'pækɪŋ〕*n*. 包裝

crude〔krud〕*adj*. 草率的；粗糙的　　apology〔ə'pɑlədʒɪ〕*n*. 道歉

Hint Bank－貨運實用語彙

- *bill of clearance* 出港申報書　　*supply station* 供應站
- *considerate service* 服務週到
- breakdown〔'brek,daʊn〕*n*. 故障
- *non returnable* 概不退換　　*mail order* 郵購
- *sales agency* 分銷處　　*suggestion box* 意見箱
- *packer's slip* 包裝標籤　　*commercial credit* 商業信用

4. Would you confirm the dispatch date?

你確定發送日期嗎？

● **One Point Advice**

有些企業公司非常重視**交貨日期**。甚至在契約上，特別註明對於延遲交貨的**罰金**（ ***penalty*** ）付款條件。相反地，若是在交貨日期以前交貨，也有獎勵的規定。一般常見的**付款條件**（ ***terms of payment*** ）有 ***cash with order*** （**訂購付款**） ***cash on delivery*** （**交貨付款**）兩種。

外國人： ***Would you confirm the order dispatch date？***

你確定訂單發送日期嗎？

⇨ *What is the dispatch date...？* 發送日期是何時…？

⇨ *I'd like to confirm the dispatch date...*

我想確定一下發送日期…

⇨ *Could you reconfirm the shipping date？*

你能否再確定一下裝船的日期？

中國人： Certainly. What's your order number？

當然。你的訂單號碼多少？

Yes, they'll be sent next week.

是的，下星期就會送出去。

⇨ *They're scheduled to be sent on May the tenth*

預計是五月十日送出。

⇨ *They were shipped...* 已裝船…

外國人： They're due to arrive in Seattle on the tenth of June？

應該會在六月十日到達西雅圖嗎？

中國人：Sure, they should arrive. 當然，應該會到。

外國人：***By the way***, may I make one change in the order?

那麼，我可以在訂單上做個修正嗎？

外國人：I'll check to see if it's possible.

我得查查看可不可能。

● Notes

confirm〔kən′fɝm〕*v.* 確定　　***dispatch day*** 發送日期

schedule〔′skɛdʒul〕*v.* 預定　　***be due to*** 應該會；預定的

Hint Bank－貨運實用語彙

- *sales by sample* 樣品交易　　*market report* 市場報告
- *export quarantine* 出口檢疫
- *instalment payment* 分期付款
- *instalment shipment* 分批裝船
- *date of shipment* 裝船日期
- *deferred payment* 延付貨款

5. What can you do to solve the matter?

你如何解決這件事？

● **One Point Advice**

當顧客抱怨產品有**瑕疵**（***defective***）時，第一步就是先了解損壞的**程度、內容**及**賠償**要求等事實，再冷靜的處理。這時如果你的英文溝通能力不佳，可能會引起其它的誤會，而使情況變的更糟。因此在顧客問起：***What can you do to solve the matter***？之前，必須熟練以下的句型。

顧　客：Upon opening the shipment, we found five pieces were broken. 打開船貨時，我們發現有五件破損了。

⇨ *The delivered goods are short by twenty units...*

裝運的貨物少了二十件…

⇨ *The machines are out of order...*

機器故障了…

How can we solve this matter?

我們該如何解決這件事？

Could you send replacements at once?

你們能否立刻送替換品來？

⇨ *We request urgent replacement of...*

我們要求緊急替換…

廠　商：Certainly. We'll arrange for shipping of replacements immediately.

當然。我們會馬上安排替換品的裝船。

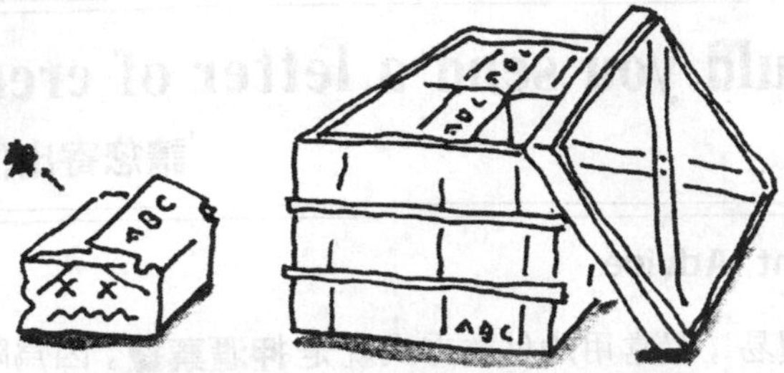

▷ *I'll have the replacements shipped today.*
我今天就將替換品裝船。

▷ *We are sending the articles you require by air mail...* 我們正以航空郵寄你所要求的物件。

We'll take all possible steps to prevent such a mistake from happening again.

我們將採取所有可能的措施，以防止再發生這種錯誤。

● Notes

unit〔'junɪt〕*n.* 單件　replacement〔rɪ'plesmənt〕*n.* 替換品
request〔rɪ'kwɛst〕*v.* 要求　urgent〔'ɝdʒənt〕*adj.* 緊急的
arrange〔ə'rendʒ〕*v.* 安排　prevent〔prɪ'vɛnt〕*v.* 防止

Hint Bank —貨運實用語彙

- *certificate of origin* 產地證明書
- *charter party* 租船契約　*purchasing power* 購買力
- *notice of damage* 損毀通知　*freight broker* 運貨行
- *beware of imitators* 防止假冒
- *dealing in future* 期貨　*trade discount* 同業折扣

6. Would you send a letter of credit?

請您寄出信用狀好嗎？

● **One Point Advice**

進出口貿易，最常用的付款方式就是**押滙票據**，因爲附有**信用狀**(***credit letter***)的買賣，即使進口商拒絕付款，開設信用狀的銀行也會保證付起責任，所以對出口商而言非常安全。信用狀的當事人有委託開狀人(即指進口商 ***importer***)、開狀銀行(***issuing bank***)、受益人(即出口商 ***exporter***)和押滙銀行(***negotiating bank***)。

中國人： We have not received ***the letter of credit*** covering your order. 我們沒有收到附上你的訂單的信用狀。
Would you send it? Without your letter of credit, we can't negotiate your bills.
你寄了嗎？沒有你的信用狀，我們便無法押滙。

⇨ *We'd like you to open a letter of credit...*
我們希望你開一張信用狀…

⇨ *We'll send you a statement of your credit.*
我們會寄給你一份信用狀。

⇨ *Would you send us a check to settle the balance?*
你能寄一張支票給我們補足餘額嗎？

外國人： ***I'm very sorry for the delay*** in opening the letter of credit, but we finally obtained it on March the seventh. It was mailed to you yesterday.
我很抱歉躭誤了開信用狀的時間，但我終於在三月七日拿到了。昨天已經寄給你了。

➪ *We've remitted one million dollars to you through the M. Bank.*

我們已經經由M銀行滙寄了一百萬美元給你。

➪ *We've arranged payment of your invoice.*

我們已經安排好你的發票的支付。

● **Notes**

letter of credit 信用狀

balance〔'bæləns〕*n.* 餘額

remit〔rɪ'mɪt〕*v.* 滙寄

negotiate〔nɪ'goʃɪ,et〕*v.*（證券、票據等）流通；兌換

obtain〔əb'ten〕*v.* 拿到；獲得

invoice〔'ɪnvɔɪs〕*n.* 發票

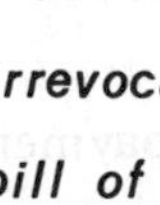

Hint Bank－滙票和信用狀實用語彙

- *bank draft* 銀行滙票　　*sight bill* 即期滙票
- *revocable letter of credit* 可取銷信用狀
- *irrevocable letter of credit* 不可取銷信用狀
- *bill of exchange* 滙票　　*time bill* 遠期滙票

7. Let's get down to business.

讓我們開始談生意。

● One Point Advice

雙方訂立契約書的第一步，就是要確認契約的型態，是本人對本人的**買賣契約**（ ***sales contract*** ），還是本人對代理商**代理契約**（ ***agency contract*** ）。前者則對日後產品的銷售負全責，若為後者，則權利的劃分必須明確。一般的契約書都具有下列各項基本交易條件：①商品名稱②交貨日期③數量④價格⑤交貨方式⑥保險⑦付款條件。

中國人： Let's ***get down to business***, shall we？
讓我們開始談生意，好嗎？
➪ *Shall we begin*？我們可以開始了嗎？

外國人： Well, where shall we start？嗯，我們該由哪兒開始？
➪ *How shall we proceed*？我們如何開始進行？
➪ *How shall we begin*？我們如何開始？

中國人： We'd like to discuss an agency contract with you.
我們想與你討論訂立代理契約的事宜。
We hope to reach an agreement as soon as possible.
我們希望儘快達成協定。

外國人： I see. We'd like to discuss the terms of payment in more detail.
我明白。我們想進一步討論付款條件。

中國人：Let me see...I think I can offer you a good price.
我看看…我想我可提供你一個好價錢。
But first let me talk to our boss on the phone.
但得先讓我打電話告訴我老板。

....

Here is our offer. 這是我們的出價。

外國人：Hmm...With a 30% down payment…
嗯…訂金百分之三十。

● Notes

proceed〔prə'sid〕*v.* 開始進行　　discuss〔dɪ'skʌs〕*v.* 討論
terms of payment 付款條件　　offer〔'ɔfɚ, 'ɑfɚ〕*v.* 提供
down payment 訂金

Hint Bank－契約交易實用語彙

- *bid bonds* 招標保證金　*trading partner* 貿易合夥人
- *RFQ* 要求報價（＝*request for quotation*）
- *bid opening procedures* 開標手續
- *sales contract* 銷售契約
- *formal contract* 正式契約
- *purchase contract* 購買契約
- *free alongside ship* 船邊交貨
- *retention money* 保留金　*carriage paid* 運費已付
- objection〔əb'dʒɛkʃən〕*n.* 異議　*charter party* 租船契約

8. Preparing a draft of the contract

準備草擬契約草稿

● **One Point Advice**

正式擬定契約之前，還需注意討論下列問題：契約期間、變更與毀約的責任、傭金、免責事項、滙款、信用狀、發生糾紛時的**仲裁方式**等。如果對於適用的法律條文有疑問時，最好能馬上請教律師（ ***lawyer*** ）。契約所牽涉的問題非常多，若可先拿一份**標準契約格式**（ ***standard contract*** ）作參考，按步就班來討論，就方便多了。

外國人： Shall we ***draw up a draft*** of the contract？

我們是否該擬一份契約草案？

Do you have a sample？你有樣本嗎？

中國人： This is our standard contract.

這是我們的標準契約。

Have you ever seen it？你看過了嗎？

外國人： No, not until now. 不，目前還沒有。

How about preparing a draft ***according to*** your standard contract？根據你們的標準契約來準備一份草案如何？

中國人： Fine. Now, how long will the contract last？

好。那麼，這契約將持續多久呢？

⇨ *How long shall we make the contract for*？

這契約將持續多久呢？

外國人： Initially？ I would suggest one year.

開始呢？我提議一年。

中國人： I'm afraid that one year is too short.

我怕一年太短了。

This contract must be valid for at least three years.

契約必須至少依法有效三年。

外國人： If everything's going satisfactorily, it could be extended for two years. 如果一切進行得令人滿意,可以再延長兩年。

● Notes

draw up 草擬　draft〔dræft〕*n.* 草案；草稿

prepare〔prɪ'pɛr〕*v.* 準備　valid〔'vælɪd〕*adj.* 依法有效的

satisfactorily〔,sætɪs'fæktərɪlɪ〕*adv.* 令人滿意地　extend〔ɪk'stɛnd〕*v.* 延長

Hint Bank — 契約交易實用語彙

- *contract provisions* 契約條款　*sales note* 銷售確認書
- commission〔kə'mɪʃən〕*n.* 傭金　*fixed price* 定價
- *payment provisions* 支付條款　*after sight* 見票後
- *termination of an agreement* 契約期滿
- *all contract documents* 所有契約文件
- *purchase note* 購買確認書
- *Force Majeure* 不可抗力
- *due date* 支付日期
- *proforma invoice* 估價發票

9. Let me think it over.

讓我考慮一下。

● **One Point Advice**

面對面的商定契約內容時，一定會碰到雙方都不願意讓步的問題，這時將最後的決定權,推給你的上司是最好的緩衝方式: ***It's impossible for me to give a definite answer now.*** or ***Let me talk to my boss about your offer.*** 這種**折衝戰術**往往都能奏效，讓對方在權衡得失之後，仍然會稍微讓步。

外國人：This is something we have to consider.

這事我們必須考慮。

Let me think it over, please. 請讓我考慮考慮。

It's impossible for me to give a definite answer now.

我現在不能給你明確的答覆。

➩ *I can't reach a decision by myself.*

我無法自己做決定。

➩ *I don't have the authority to decide this alone.*

我沒有權力自己決定。

中國人：These are our usual terms. Please understand our situation. 這是我們的一般條例。請體諒我們的處境。

We operate on a ***cash-with-order basis*** for the down-payment. I'd like to hear your ideas about this.

我們對頭期款施行現金支付的原則。我想聽聽你對這的看法。

◇ *What's your opinion ?* 你的意見如何？

◇ *Let me have your views on this.*

讓我聽聽你對這的看法。

外國人：A 30％ downpayment is a little stiff for us.

百分之三十的頭期款對我們來說有點困難。

中國人：If you pay within ten days, we allow a 1％ discount.

如果你們在十天內支付，我們允許百分之一的折扣。

外國人：From the total price? Well, ***let me talk to my boss about your offer.***

是總價嗎？嗯，讓我和老板談談你的提議。

◇ *I need time to consult with my boss.*

我需要時間問問老板。

● Notes

consider〔kən'sɪdɚ〕*v.* 考慮　impossible〔ɪm'pɑsəbl̩〕*adj.* 不可能的

definite〔'dɛfənɪt〕*adj.* 明確的　authority〔ə'θɔrətɪ〕*n.* 權力；權限

usual terms 一般條例　operate〔'ɑpə,ret〕*v.* 施行

view〔vju〕*n.* 看法；意見　stiff〔stɪf〕*adj.* 困難；嚴苛

discount〔'dɪskaʊnt〕*n.* 折扣

Hint Bank—契約交易實用語彙

- *warranty period* 保障期限　*breach of contract* 違約
- *CIF* 起岸價（＝*cost*, *insurance* & *freight*）
- *nonfulfillment of contract* 不履行契約
- indemnity〔ɪn'dɛmnətɪ〕*n.* 賠償金

10. Aren't you satisfied with the terms?

您對條款不滿意嗎？

● **One Point Advice**

契約的訂定，有時並不如期望中那麼順利。雙方代表可能在某個關鍵問題上談不攏，而無法達成協議。俗話說：「買賣不成仁義在」，若是鬧得不歡而散，也會造成日後再度合作的不便。這時你若能**禮貌**地說：***I'm really sorry but I have to leave.*** 就可適宜地表達你的態度和立場，而不失風度。

外國人： We have some points we need to explore further.

我們有幾點需要更深入研究。

➪ *There are some points that need to be worked out.*

有幾點需要詳細計畫的。

➪ *There is some necessity for discussion...*

有討論的必要…

中國人： ***Aren't you satisfied with*** the terms of payment?

你對付款的條文不滿意嗎？

外國人： No, not entirely. 是的，不完全滿意。

The terms of payment are too severe.

付款的條文太嚴苛。

By the way, Mr. Wang, to what companies did you supply these components?

此外，王先生，你們將這些組合零件提供給什麼公司呢？

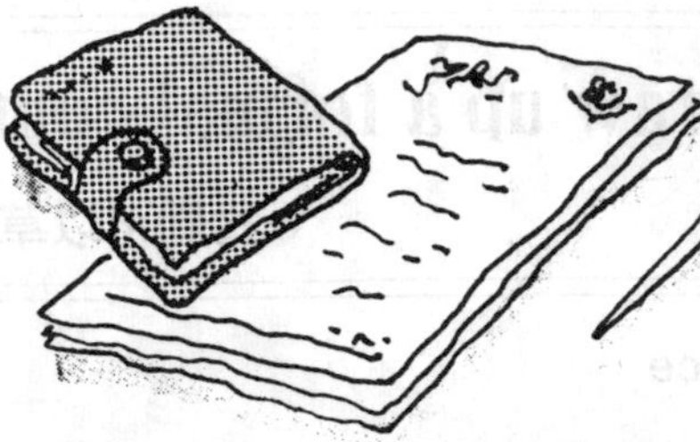

中國人： I'm sorry, I can't give you that information.

抱歉，我無法告訴你那項消息。

You wouldn't want other companies to know what components you are using, would you?

你不會希望其他公司知道你用什麼組合零件，是不是？

外國人： Yes, you're right. 是的。

➪ *I understand your concern.* 我了解你的顧慮。

Well, ***I'm really sorry but I have to leave.***

哦，很抱歉我必須離開了。

➪ *Please excuse me for a moment.*

請原諒我離開一會兒。

● **Notes**

explore〔ɪk'splor, -'splɔr〕*v.* 研究；探討　　severe〔sə'vɪr〕*adj.* 嚴苛的

Hint Bank－契約交易實用語彙

· *price list* 價目表　　attorney〔ə'tɝnɪ〕*n.* 代理人；律師

· *date of dispatch* 遞出的日期　　*bill of lading* 提單

· arbitration〔,ɑrbə'treʃən〕*n.* 仲裁

11. We can draw up a formal contract.

我們可以草擬一份正式契約。

● **One Point Advice**

正式承作契約書時，除了要注意內容的**合法性**（ ***legality*** ）之外，還要注意下列各點(1)詞句力求**簡短、直接**(2)相關的條文不可互相**矛盾**(3)少用**被動式**，時態以**現在式**爲主(4)明確的列出法律行爲的**證據**（ ***evidence*** ）。另外 ***feel free to*** ～的句型，值得上班族熟記。

中國人： If everything is satisfactory, we can draw up a formal contract.

如果一切都滿意了，我們可以擬定一份正式契約。

外國人： I'll ***look over*** this contract and have my president look at it. 我先看過一遍契約後，再讓我們董事長看。

中國人： When will the contract papers be ready?

契約文件何時可準備好？

⇨ ***When can we sign it?***

我們什麼時候簽署？

外國人： We expect to make a formal contract by the end of this month. 我們希望在月底前，完成一份正式契約。

中國人： Please ***feel free to*** ask me any questions which you may have on your mind.

你有什麼疑問的話，請儘管來問我。

➪ *Feel free to drop by our office any time.*

任何時候歡迎到我辦公室來。

外國人： I'll let you know if anything important happens.

如果有什麼重要的事，我會讓你知道的。

● Notes

look over 看看；檢討　ready〔ˈrɛdɪ〕*adj.* 準備好的

president〔ˈprɛzədənt〕*n.* 董事長　***contract papers*** 契約文件

Hint Bank—契約交易實用語彙

- *in witness whereof* 以資證明　*trade mark* 商標
- inspection〔ɪnˈspɛkʃən〕*n.* 檢驗　*war risk* 兵險
- brand〔brænd〕*n.* 品牌
- *attest principals* 立證據本人
- *attest agents* 立證據代理商
- duplicate〔ˈdjupləkɪt〕*n.* 相同的東西；副本
- *port of shipment* 裝貨港

12. Concluding the contract

完成契約

● **One Point Advice**

契約中，表示確切的日期用 ***on***，如 ***on May 1***（在五月一日當天）。表示「**到某月某日之前**」則用 ***by*** 或 ***before*** 。***by*** 不包括**當天**，如 ***by May 1***（到五月一日之前）就不包括五月一日，指到 ***April 30*** 爲止 。***from May 1***，亦不包括當天，意指從 ***May 2*** 開始 。若用 ***commencing*** 則包括當天。這些介係詞的用法，事先須多加注意，以避免日後發生解釋上的麻煩 。

中國人：Is it possible to ***conclude the contract*** this month?
有可能在這個月訂立契約嗎？

外國人：Yes, I'll send you the contract note ***by the end of this month***. 是的，月底前我會把契約通知送交給你 。

中國人：That's fine. At last, we are both satisfied.
很好 。終於，我們雙方都滿意了 。
➩ *We're in agreement on all points.*
我們對所有項目都意見一致 。
I would like you to let us have the contract as soon as possible. 我希望你能儘速讓我們訂約 。

外國人：***Is it possible to change the details*** of the contract after it's been made?
簽約後還有可能改變契約的細目嗎？

中國人：The contract can be cancelled by mutual agreement and with three months' notice it can be annulled.
契約可以經雙方協議後取消，且經三個月的公告，即可廢止。

外國人：Well, thank you very much, Mr. Wang. I'll be seeing you. 嗯，非常謝謝你，王先生。再見。
⇨ *Let's call it a day*. 讓我們做個結束吧。

中國人：Thank you, Mr. Brown. Good-bye.
謝謝你，布朗先生。再見。

● Notes

conclude〔kən'klud〕*v*. 結束；決定　cancel〔'kænsl̩〕*v*. 取消
mutual〔mjutʃuəl〕*adj*. 相互的　notice〔'notɪs〕*n*. 公告　annul〔ə'nʌl〕*v*. 廢止

Hint Bank－契約交易實用語彙

- termination〔,tɝmə'neʃən〕*n*. 終止
- *marine insurance* 海上保險　*basis price* 基本價格
- *bill of dishonor* 空頭支票　*bottom price* 底價

13. Sorry, I'm late.

抱歉, 我遲到了。

● **One Point Advice**

無論是參加宴會，會議或與人相約，最好能準時到達。如果必須遲到，最好能說明理由。尤其是會議已在進行中時，若不說 ***Sorry for being late***，就貿然闖入，則非常不禮貌。這時主人可能會對你說 ***Actually we're just getting down to business.***（事實上，我們才剛開始進入正題。），以表示原諒你的遲到。

中國人：***Sorry, I'm late.*** 抱歉，我遲到了。

- *Sorry, I kept you waiting.* 抱歉，讓你久等了。
- *Sorry for being late.* 抱歉，我遲到了。
- *Forgive us for being late.* 請原諒我們遲到了。

中國人：That's all right. 沒關係。

- *No problem.* 沒關係。
- *That's O.K.* 沒關係。

We've just started. 我們才剛開始。

⇨ *Actually we're just getting down to business.*

事實上，我們才剛開始進入正題。

⇨ *We just got here ourselves.* 我們也才剛開始。

中國人： That's good. 那很好。

⇨ *I'm relieved to hear that.*

聽你那麼說，我覺得比較放心了。

外國人： Don't worry about it. 別擔心。

● **Notes**

keep someone waiting 讓某人久等　　forgive〔fə'gɪv〕*v.* 原諒
get down to business 進入正題　　***be relieved*** 感到放心

Hint Bank－遲到的理由

- The traffic was completely jammed this morning.
  今天早上塞車很厲害。
- I forgot to set my alarm last night.
  昨天晚上我忘記上鬧鐘了。
- When I was about to leave, one of my customers dropped in on me. 我正要出來時，我的一位客戶來找我。
- I had trouble finding your meeting hall.
  我好不容易才找到你們的會議廳。

14. Going to a home party

參加家庭宴會

● **One Point Advice**

歐美人士多半喜歡在自己的家中舉行宴會，因此在參加之前，一定要熟記一些應對用語。例如在剛**抵達**時，先表示感謝對方誠意的邀請：***It was very kind of you to invite us***. 而在宴會**進行中**，適時的一句：***You look perfect in that dress***. 就可立即打開話匣子了。當然宴會**結束**後可別忘了向主人說：***I really enjoyed the party this evening***.

中國人：Hello！ Here we are. 嗨！我們來了。

外國人：***Hi！ It's been a long time***. 嗨！好久不見。

How've you been? Come on in. 近來如何？請進。

➪ *Please come in*. 請進。

➪ *Come right in*. 請進。

中國人：***Thank you. I've been busy. How about you***?

謝謝。我一直很忙。你呢？

外國人：***Pretty busy, too. Just recently I was thinking that we should get together***.

也很忙。最近我想到我們應該聚聚了。

Did you have any trouble finding us?

你找我們家的時候，有沒有遇到什麼麻煩？

➪ *Any problems getting here*? 到這裡來有沒有困難？

中國人：No. Your directions were great.

沒有。你的說明很清楚。

⇨ *No, none at all.* 不，一點也沒有。

外國人：Please make yourself at home. 請不要拘束。

⇨ *Make yourself comfortable.* 儘量讓自己覺得舒服些。

I'd like you to meet my wife, Lily. 見見我太太,莉莉。

⇨ *This is Lily, my wife.* 這是莉莉，我太太。

● **Notes**

get together 聚會；聚集 trouble〔ˈtrʌbl̩〕*n.* 困難

make oneself at home 請某人不要拘束

Hint Bank—宴會洋酒名稱

· claret〔ˈklærət〕*n.* 紅葡萄酒

· hock〔hɑk〕*n.* 白葡萄酒 gin〔dʒɪn〕*n.* 杜松子酒

· vodka〔ˈvɑdkɑ〕*n.* 伏爾加酒 ***malt liquor*** 麥芽酒

· champagne〔ʃæmˈpen〕*n.* 香檳

· whisky〔ˈhwɪskɪ〕*n.* 威士忌酒

15. The party is over.

宴會結束。

● One Point Advice

宴會結束時，主人多半會到門口送客。這時，你必須說些**感謝**或**讚美**的話來表示你的謝意。***Thanks for everything***.（感謝你所做的一切。）或***The dinner was just delicious***.（晚餐非常美味可口。）皆爲適宜的用語。身爲主人也不妨以***We enjoyed having you***.（我們很高興你能來。）來回答。

中國人： ***Thanks for everything***. It was a wonderful evening.

非常感謝你所做的一切。這眞是美好的一夜。

The dinner was just delicious. 晚餐非常美味可口。

▷ *Thank you so much. I had a nice time.*

非常感謝，我覺得很愉快。

▷ *I had a wonderful time*. 我覺得很愉快。

▷ *I especially enjoyed that dinner*.

我尤其喜歡那頓晚餐。

外國人： We are glad to hear that. ***We certainly enjoyed having you over***. 我們很高興聽你這麼說。當然我們也很高興你能來。

▷ *We enjoyed having you*. 我們很高興你能來。

▷ *It was our pleasure*. 這是我們的榮幸。

You must come again sometime.

改天你一定要再來。

中國人：Thank you. Let's get together again.

謝謝你。讓我們再聚一聚。

We would like to have you visit us sometime ***in the near future***. 我們希望最近你也能到舍下來。

➪ *We have to do this again.* 我們必須再聚一聚。

➪ *We'll do it again soon.* 我們不久還要再聚。

Goodbye. ***We'll be seeing you soon.*** 再見，不久見。

● Notes

delicious〔dɪˈlɪʃəs〕*adj.* 美味可口的　　***in the near future*** 不久的將來；最近

Hint Bank 一宴會飲酒用語

- *drinking contest* 划拳吃酒　　*propose a toast* 敬一杯
- refill〔rɪˈfɪl〕*v.* 再倒一杯　　*bottoms up* 一飲而盡
- *capacity for wine* 酒量　　*tuck in* 暢飲
- *highly intoxicated* 沈醉　　drunkard〔ˈdrʌŋkɚd〕*n.* 醉漢

16. Be the life of the party.

不當宴會壁花。

● One Point Advice

不當壁花的七原則：

(1) **積極派的說話方式**

在歐美社會中，有一句鐵律：***If you don't speak, you are nobody.***（如果你不說話，你就不存在）。因此在社交應酬時，一定要掌握語言這項利器，就是表現出 ***aggressive*** 的態度也無妨。

(2) **與對方站在同等的立場**

在與外國人應對說話時，沒有必要對他們表示畏縮或緊張（tense），重要的是要有**自主**的行動，把持自己的**立場**。***Think on your own.*** 不要受他人的意見所左右。

(3) **比起流暢的英語，寧以內容取勝**

說得流暢，但內容膚淺與寡言卻言之有物的人相比，顯然是後者爲佳。在歐美社會中，常以談話的內容來評斷你的程度。

(4) **以自己拿手的話題來主導會話的進行**

與外國人說話時，不要一味猛點頭附和對方。將自己擅長的主題帶入會話中，有助於彼此感情的建立。

(5) **讓球運轉**（***keep the ball rolling***）

不要忽略了對方所說的普通話題，要進一步找出對方的意見和感想。如果光說 ***I see*** 或 ***yes***，只會中斷會話的進行。另外，"***why***"最好也少用爲妙。

(6) **發揮幽默的精神**

在人際摩擦頻繁的商場上，幽默是舒解緊張氣氛的良藥。因此在應酬時，能博君一笑才是一流的人物。

(7) **演說三原則：**

informative（資料豐富），***persuasive***（有說服力），***entertaining***（娛樂性）——從日常生活會話到正式宴會的演說，都要予以注意。

● **以星座爲話題**

◇ What is your astrological sign? 你是什麼星座？

◇ I'm a Cancer. 我是巨蟹座。

• **Notes**

astrological sign 星座　Cancer〔ˈkænsɚ〕*n.* 巨蟹座

● **以血型爲話題**

◇ What is your ***bloodtype***? 你是什麼血型？

◇ I'm a type O blood person. 我是O型。

● **以吃爲話題**

◇ What is your favorite food and why?
你最喜歡的食物是什麼，爲什麼？

◇ ***Have you ever heard*** "Ching & Han Royal Dynasty Feast"?
你聽過「滿漢全席」嗎？

◇ Do you like the food served today? 你喜歡今天的菜色嗎？

◇ I know a restaurant known for their seafood. You must go there and taste it.
我知道一家以海鮮聞名的餐廳。你一定要去嚐嚐看。

● **Notes**

Ching & Han Royal Dynasty Feast 滿漢全席

● 以健康爲話題

◇ I'm getting the middle-age spread. 我開始像中年人一樣發福了。

◇ You can pinch an inch. 你小腹的脂肪有一吋厚。

● **Notes**

pinch〔pɪntʃ〕*v.* 夾；擰　　***middle-age spread*** 中年發福

● 以休閒活動爲話題

◇ What kind of sports do you enjoy? 你喜歡哪種運動？

◇ I play golf. 我打高爾夫球。

◇ Why don't we go fishing sometime, then?
找個時間去釣魚，如何？

◇ In Taiwan, you are often asked to display your secret talents at parties. 在台灣，你常常在宴會中，被要求展示你的秘密才華。

◇ I hear even President Reagan pumps iron every day.
據說雷根總統也每天做健身運動。

● 以社會現象爲話題

◇ Do you think you're religious? 你有宗教信仰嗎？

◇ What do you mean by "religious"? 你所說的宗教信仰是什麼意思?

◇ What do you think are the causes of school violence?
你認爲校園暴力的原因是什麼？

◇ With that high divorce rate, how do Americans view marriage?
以那麼高的離婚率，美國人是如何看待婚姻的？

◇ ***This is my pet theory.*** 這是我得意的論調。

● Notes

religious〔rɪˈlɪdʒəs〕*adj.* 有宗教信仰的；宗教的

Hint Bank－星座名稱

- Aries〔ˈɛrɪ,iz〕*n.* 牡羊座 3/21～4/19
- Taurus〔ˈtɔrəs〕*n.* 牡牛座 4/20～5/20
- Gemini〔ˈdʒɛmə,naɪ〕*n.* 雙子座 5/21～6/21
- Cancer〔ˈkænsɚ〕*n.* 巨蟹座 6/22～7/22
- Leo〔ˈlio〕*n.* 獅子座 7/23～8/22
- Virgo〔ˈvɝgo〕*n.* 處女座 8/23～9/22
- Libra〔ˈlaɪbrə〕*n.* 天秤座 9/23～10/23
- Scorpio〔ˈskɔrpɪ,o〕*n.* 天蠍座 10/24～11/22
- Sagittarius〔,sædʒɪˈtɛrɪəs〕*n.* 射手座 11/23～12/21
- Capricorn〔ˈkæprɪ,kɔrn〕*n.* 山羊座 12/22～1/19
- Aquarius〔əˈkwɛrɪəs〕*n.* 水瓶座 1/20～2/18
- Pisces〔ˈpɪsiz〕*n.* 雙魚座 2/19～3/20

17. Go happily to the party.

快樂地參加宴會。

● **One Point Advice**

(1) 快樂地參加宴會基本原則

① 做個 good mixer（善於交際的人）

宴會的目的，在於與老朋友敍舊和認識新朋友。並且可擴大交際範圍和情報來源。因此不要只和認識的人聚集在一起，要儘量結識新朋友，做個會掌握**氣氛**的 good mixer。

② 被討厭的人纏住該怎麼辦？

可向他介紹**路過**的朋友，告訴他你要拿飲料。也可以問他說“***Can I get you a drink*** ?”藉故離去。

③ 聲音宏量，擧止合宜

要訓練在嘈雜的環境中，將自己的聲音傳得很遠。雖然太大聲會打擾到別人，但中國人總是怕說錯英語而不敢開口，或說話聲音很小，讓人不易聽懂。另外在宴會中要擧止合宜，不必過份謙卑客氣，也不必擺架子，宴會就是要輕鬆愉快才好。

④ 全場都是陌生人時…

如果宴會中全是陌生人時，可請主人幫你介紹新朋友。以某人爲目標向他接近也可以。記得在自我介紹時，要清楚地告訴對方你的**全名**。

⑤ 準備笑話和獨特的話題

在宴會中，最好不要說生意上的話題，更不要只顧吃喝而冷落了一旁的朋友。適當的**笑話**可以打破僵局，成爲會話的開始。臨機應變的笑話，其實是平時努力累積的結果。「你去過卡拉OK嗎?」像這類閒談式的問話，也可慢慢發展成為談話的話題。

⑥ **常常提到對方的名字**

外國人的名字很難一下子就記住。但在宴會中可將對方的名字寫在紙上，並在會話中反覆提到對方的名字，這在歐美是一種禮儀。

⑦ **離席時的道謝要具體**

宴會結束時，別忘向女主人道謝，可以擺飾的花真美，菜餚的可口或女主人的魅力等加以讚美。同時不要忘了感謝男主人。你可說：***I really enjoyed the party this evening.***

⑧ **用 follow-up 來抓住生意機會**

在宴會中對有希望成為生意伙伴的人，最好能積極地和他約定日後見面事宜。在宴會中的口頭承諾，日後一定會有所反應的。

(2) **宴會的種類**

① ***dinner party***（**晚宴**）

以吃晚餐為主的宴會，並附有雞尾酒等飲料。座席有預先安排好。

② ***cocktail party***（**雞尾酒會**）

以自助式的餐點為主，自由取食。宴會中每人或坐或站，手持玻璃酒杯，到處來回走動地交談。

③ ***reception***〔rɪˈsɛpʃən〕***n.***（**歡迎會**）

以歡迎招待某些人為主的宴會。開始和結束時都會有簡短的演說致詞，說明介紹這次宴會的來賓。

④ ***ball***〔bɔl〕***n.***（**舞會**）

社交性色彩極濃的舞會。參加者多必盛裝，常在國際會議後舉行。

⑤ ***barbecue party***（**烤肉餐會**）

在戶外舉行的烤肉餐會。主食以漢堡、牛排等燒烤類爲主。通常在男士們的指導下烹調餐食。如在澳洲，肉的烹煮是男士們的工作。

⑥ ***open house party***（**開放式宴會**）

在家中舉行的開放式宴會。一次招待很多人，有比預定開始的時間晚一點去的習慣。

⑦ ***potluck party***（**便餐會**）

由參加的人各自帶現成的食物來。是一種氣氛輕鬆的餐會，大家都不讓主人費心。

● 見面寒暄用語

◇ Thank you very much for your kind arrangement.
非常感謝你親切的安排。

◇ This is to celebrate your getting well.
這是慶祝你的病情好轉。

◇ ***Thank you for giving us such a warm greeting.***
謝謝你給我們如此溫暖的問候。

◇ I'm so glad you could come. 我很高興你能來。

◇ ***It was very kind of you*** to invite us. 你眞親切，邀請我們。

◇ Good evening, Mr. Johnson. Thank you for inviting me.
晚安，強生先生。謝謝你邀請我。

◇ Pleased (Glad, Nice) to meet you, Mr. Clark.
很高興遇見你，克拉克先生。

● 介紹用語

◇ Hello. ***May I introduce myself***? My name is…… .
嗨。我可以自我介紹嗎？我的名字是……。

◇ Mr. Morris, this is Mr. Wang of the Taipei Motor Company of Taiwan. 墨利斯先生，這位是台灣台北汽車公司的王先生。

◇ How do you do, Mr. Morris, ***I'm very happy to meet you.***
你好，墨利斯先生，非常高興認識你。

◇ This is George Mooney, who is doing all those fascinating heart transplants.
這位就是做過多次成功心臟移植手術的喬治·慕尼先生。

◇ This is Thomas Morris, the new buyer in the jewelry department. 這位是湯瑪斯·墨利斯，珠寶部門新的採購員。

◇ This is Joyce Harvey, who has become an avid cyclist lately.
這位是最近成爲衆所熱望的自行車選手喬伊斯·哈維。

◇ This is Bob Scherer, who has just moved to town.
這位是剛搬到城裏的鮑伯·司奇洛。

◇ This is Miss Judy Anton, who is going to sit next to you tonight. She just came back from England.
這是今晚將要坐在你旁邊的茱蒂·安頓小姐。她剛從英國回來。

◇ Mr. Carolan, I want you to see my colleague, Mr. Lee, the sales manager of the Taipei office.
卡若南先生，我希望你見見我的同事李先生，台北分公司的銷售經理。

◇ Ah, you are Mr. Morris. I've always wanted to meet you.
噢！您是墨利斯先生。我早就想認識您了。

● **Notes**

heart transplant 心臟移植手術　jewelry〔'dʒuəlrɪ〕*n.* 珠寶
avid〔'ævɪd〕*adj.* 熱望的　colleague〔'kɑlig〕*n.* 同事

● 讚美用語

◇ You look perfect in that dress, Ms. Cohen.
妳穿那件衣服看起來美極了，可漢太太。

◇ Isn't this place really beautiful? 這地方不是很漂亮嗎？

◇ Who's coming to your party? 誰將要來參加你的宴會？
Well, there's Jimmy, Rosalynn…… . 哦，有吉米，羅莎琳…。
Wow, that's quite a lineup. 哇，陣容眞龐大。

◇ I ***feel very fortunate to sit next to a charming lady like you***. 我覺得非常幸運能坐在一位像妳這般迷人的小姐旁邊。

● **Notes**

lineup〔'laɪn,ʌp〕*n.* 陣容　fortunate〔'fɔrtʃənɪt〕*adj.* 幸運的

● 尋找話題

◇ A nice party, isn't it? 很棒的宴會，不是嗎？

◇ Excuse me, have we met each other somewhere before?
對不起，我們以前曾經在別的地方見過嗎？

◇ Could it be that we've met someplace before?
我們以前見過面嗎？

◇ I don't think we've met. 我不覺得我們曾見過面。

◇ What's going on here? 這裏怎麼了?

◇ Are you Mr. Brown ***by any chance***? 你碰巧是布朗先生嗎?

• **Notes**

by chance 碰巧;偶然

• **用餐時**

◇ Can I have another piece of cake? 我可以再吃一塊蛋糕嗎?

◇ ***I don't drink as a rule***, but it's special today.
我不常喝酒,但今天特別。

◇ I find sushi irresistible. 我發覺壽司令人難以抗拒。

◇ I have a weakness for chocolate. 我對巧克力有偏好。

◇ With your stomach, you shouldn't eat or drink too much.
爲了你的胃,你不該飲食過量。

◇ ***Go easy on the whisky tonight***. 今晚,輕鬆暢飲威士忌。

◇ This brandy is smooth. It's really excellent.
這白蘭地很溫和,它眞的很棒。

◇ I'll have to let this cool a bit. I can't eat hot things.
我必須讓這個冷一下,我不能吃熱食。

◇ Have a cocktail before your meal. 用餐前來杯雞尾酒。

◇ For your health, it's better to go easy on your eating.
爲了你的健康,吃東西時最好輕鬆點。

◇ Don't worry. I don't eat much. 別擔心，我吃的不多。

◇ I'm a small eater. 我是個食量小的人。

◇ ***I can hold my liquor better than you think.***
我的酒量比你們想像中還好。

◇ Everybody, soup's on. 各位，湯來了。

• Notes

irresistible〔ˌɪrɪˈzɪstəbl̩, ˌɪrrɪ-〕*adj*. 難以抗拒的

weakness〔ˈwiknɪs〕*n*. 偏好　　***go easy*** 輕鬆一下

● 請問他人姓名時

◇ Excuse me, will you spell it out for me?
對不起，你能爲我拼出您的名字嗎？

◇ Will you write it down here? 您能將大名寫在這裏嗎？

◇ Mr. Martin Ennals, am I pronouncing it right?
馬丁・艾諾先生，我發音正確嗎？

◇ It's always difficult to remember people's names, you know.
你知道的，要記住人名總是很難的。

◇ I know I've seen that face before, ***but his name slips my mind***. 我知道我曾經見過他，可是我忘了他的名字。

◇ She is the life of the party. 她使得宴會蓬壁生輝。

• Notes

pronounce〔prəˈnaʊns〕*v*. 發音　　slip〔slɪp〕*v*. 滑掉

● 招待客人用語

◇ Be yourself at the party. 在宴會中請別拘束。

◇ ***Just bring yourself***. 請自己來，別客氣。

◇ Please sit down and make yourself at home.
請坐下，不要拘束。

◇ Mr. Chen, we seated you here. 陳先生，您請這兒坐。

◇ Meeting you here is a stroke of luck. I have something I want to talk to you about.
能在這裡遇到你，眞是意外的幸運。我正有點事要找你談談。

• Notes

make yourself at home 不要拘束　***a stroke of luck*** 意外的幸運

● follow-up 用語

◇ How about a drink after this? 宴會之後，去喝一杯如何？

◇ Would you like to join us for lunch next week?
你願意在下週和我們一起午餐嗎？

◇ I'd like to take you out for a typical Japanese dinner next time. 下次我要帶你去品嚐道地的日本料理。

● 道別用語

◇ How about some more wine? 再來一點酒如何？
No, thank you. I have to drive home. I've had enough.
不了，謝謝你。我必須開車回家。我已經喝太多了。

◇ I'm afraid I must be going. 我恐怕必須要走了。

◇ I ***really enjoyed the party this evening.***
今天下午的宴會非常愉快。

◇ Thank you for a wonderful evening. 謝謝你今天下午的招待。

◇ It was very nice meeting you. 非常高興見到你。

CHAPTER 3

商務文件面面觀

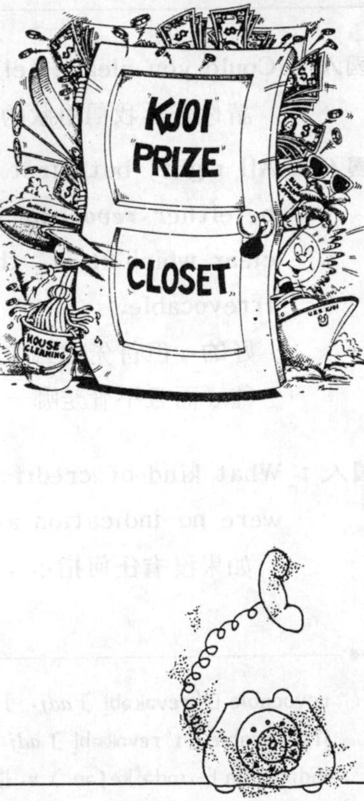

1. Types of L/C

信用狀的種類

● **One Point Advice**

商業**信用狀**（ ***Letter of credit*** ）簡稱為***L/C***。一般可分為***Revocable L/C***（可撤銷信用狀）和***Irrevocable L/C***（不可撤銷信用狀）兩種。其中以後者較為普遍，其修改（ ***amendment*** ）需經過所有信用狀當事人同意才行。

中國人： Could you please tell me about the types of credit?

請你告訴我信用狀的種類好嗎？

外國人： All right, but first you must know that credits may be either ***revocable*** or ***irrevocable***. And, it should be clear which it is, that is, whether it is revocable or irrevocable.

好的，但首先你必須了解，信用狀分為可撤銷及不可撤銷兩種。而且不管是哪一種信用狀，都應該明示。

中國人： What kind of credit would it be considered if there were no indication at all?

如果沒有任何指示，那是屬於哪一種信用狀？

** ———

revocable 〔 'rɛvəkəbl̩ 〕 *adj*. 可撤銷的

irrevocable 〔 ɪ'rɛvəkəbl̩ 〕 *adj*. 不可撤銷的

indication 〔 ˌɪndə'keʃən 〕 *n*. 指示

外國人：***If there is no such indication***, the credit will be deemed revocable ***even if the date of expiration is stipulated.***

如果沒有特別指示，將被視爲可撤銷的信用狀，縱使有規定期滿日期。

中國人：Well, what is a revocable credit, and what is the role of the bank?

嗯，什麼是可撤銷的信用狀，銀行的角色又是什麼？

外國人：A revocable credit is not legally binding between the bank or banks concerned and the beneficiary.

一份可撤銷的信用狀，在法律上，並非受銀行或相關銀行和受益人的約束。

外國人：This is because such a credit may be modified or cancelled at any time without notice to the beneficiary.

這是因爲，這種信用狀，可在任何時間，不通知受益人，而予以修改或取消。

中國人：Fine. I have one more question. ***In brief***, what is an irrevocable credit?

好。我還有一個問題。簡要地說，什麼是不可撤銷信用狀。

外國人：Well, the irrevocable credit, once issued, can be neither modified nor cancelled prior to the expiration

**

deem〔dim〕*v.* 視爲　　***date of expiration*** 期滿日期

stipulate〔'stɪpjə,let〕*v.* 規定　　beneficiary〔'bɛnə'fɪʃərɪ〕*n.* 受益人

modify〔'mɑdə,faɪ〕*v.* 修改

date without the consent of all parties concerned including the beneficiary.

嗯，不可撤銷信用狀一旦開出後，在期滿日期以前，未經過所有相關的當事人，包括受益人的同意，則無法修改或取消。

外國人：***In other words***, the issuing bank ***commits itself*** irrevocably ***to*** honour its obligation under the credit, provided that the beneficiary ***complies with*** all ***terms*** and conditions of the credit.

也就是說，如果受益人依從信用狀上的條款，開狀銀行就必須承擔兌現的責任。

中國人：Thank you very very much. You have been most helpful.

非常謝謝你。你的幫忙很大。

外國人：You're quite welcome. 不要客氣。

**

issuing bank 開狀銀行　　***commit oneself to*** 承擔

honour〔ˈɑnɚ〕*v*. 承諾兌現　　comply〔kəmˈplaɪ〕*v*. 依從

Hint Bank —工商人小格言

- The early bird catches the worm. 早起的鳥兒有蟲吃。
- Let the dead bury their dead. 既往不咎。
- Haste makes waste. 欲速則不達。
- To be not elated by success nor disturbed by failure. 勝不驕敗不餒。

2. Liabilities and Responsibilities

銀行的義務和責任

● One Point Advice

銀行若發現賣方的裝船文件和信用狀的內容不符合時，可以拒絕**議付**（***negotiate***）滙票。若因罷工、天災而必須修改信用狀時，務必立即以電文或傳眞，委託買方修改。受益人議付滙票時，可持信用狀原本和**修改部分**向銀行請求議付。

外國人：Good afternoon, Mr. Wang. 午安，王先生。

中國人：Ah, Mr. Brown. How are you today?
啊，伯朗先生。今天好嗎？

外國人：Fine, thanks, and you? 很好，謝謝你。你呢？

中國人：Fine, thank you. ***By the way***, may I ask you some questions? 很好，謝謝你。對了，我可以請教你一些問題嗎?

外國人：Sure, ***by all means***. 當然，當然。

中國人：What are the liabilities and responsibilities of banks in handling an L/C?
在處理信用狀時，銀行的義務和責任是什麼？

外國人：Well, as you probably already know, banks must examine all documents with reasonable care to ascertain

---

**

by all means 當然；一定

that they appear, ***on the face***, to be ***in accordance with*** the ***terms and conditions of the credit***.

嗯，你可能已經知道，銀行必須很仔細地檢查所有的文件，以確定文件上的文字與信用狀的條款一致。

中國人： In documentary credit operations, do all parties concerned deal in documents and not in goods?

在初步操作信用狀時，所有相關的當事人，都在文件上作業，而不是在貨物上嗎？

外國人： That's right, but I must emphasize that banks do not assume any liability or responsibility for the form, sufficiency, accuracy, genuineness, falsification or legal effect of any documents, or for the general and/or particular conditions stipulated in the documents.

是的，但我必須強調一點，銀行對於任何文件的形式，效率、準確性、眞實、僞造或法律效果，不負任何義務和責任，對於文件上所規定的一般或特別條款，也不負責。

中國人： What about in case of an error? 如果有錯誤該如何？

外國人： Well, banks naturally assume no liability or responsibility for delay, mutilation or other errors arising from the transmission of cables, telegrams or telex, or for errors in translation or interpretation of ***technical terms***.

** ————————————

on the face 在字面上　　accordance〔ə'kɔrdəns〕*n*. 一致

falsification〔,fɔlsəfə'keʃən〕*n*. 僞造

mutilation〔,mjutə'leʃən〕*n*.（電文的）錯誤　　***technical term*** 專門術語

嗯，銀行自然也不對電文或傳眞的延遲、錯誤，或專門術語的翻譯錯誤而負責。

中國人：Well then, what about cases arising from interruptions of banking business by strikes, lockouts, ***Acts of God*** (natural disasters) or ***any other causes beyond a bank's control*** ?

那麼，如果銀行因爲罷工，工廠停工，天災等不可抗力或其它銀行無法控制的原因，而中斷業務，那又如何呢？

外國人：Well, as I was going to say, banks don't assume any liability or responsibility for the consequences you mentioned.

嗯，我正要說，銀行對你所說的後果，不負任何義務或責任。

**

lockout〔'lɑk,aʊt〕*n.* 工廠停工　***Acts of God*** 不可抗力；天災

Hint Bank—工商人小格言

❖ Know your enemy and know yourself.
知己知彼百戰百勝。

❖ It's never too late to learn.
活到老學到老。

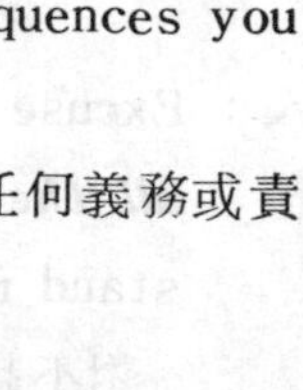

❖ Offence is the best defence.
先下手爲強。

3. Shipping Documents 1

裝船文件 1

● **One Point Advice**

裝船基本三文件（ ***three basic shipping documents*** ）

◇ ***commercial invoice*** ⇨ 商業發票

◇ ***bill of lading*** ⇨ 提單（簡稱爲***B/L***）

◇ ***insurance policy*** ⇨ 保險單（簡稱爲***I/P***）

中國人： Excuse me, Mr. Brown, but ***I'd like to thank you for all the help you've given me.*** Thanks to you, I understand much more now about credits than before.

對不起，伯朗先生，但我要感謝你對我的幫忙。謝謝你。我現在對於信用狀，比以前更了解了。

外國人： It's my pleasure, Mr. Wang. Please feel free to contact me anytime. ***By the way***, how is your new section?

王先生，這是我的榮幸。請別客氣，儘量來找我。對了，你的新部門如何？

中國人： Busy! Very, very busy. Well, Mr. Brown, could you explain to me about the shipping documents today?

忙！非常、非常忙碌。嗯，伯朗先生，你今天可否爲我說明裝船文件的事宜？

外國人： Yes, certainly. The main shipping documents usually required in the credit transactions are the ***commercial invoice, bill of lading, and insurance policy.***

當然可以。在信用狀業務中，所需的主要裝船文件有：商業發票、提單、和保險單。

中國人： I see. They are the so-called "three basic shipping documents," aren't they?

我知道。它們是「裝船基本三文件」，不是嗎？

外國人： That's right. And various other documents, such as a ***certificate of origin***, ***weight list***, ***packing list***, and ***inspection certificate*** may also be required depending upon the buyer's country and the sales contract between buyer and seller.

沒錯。其它各種文件，如原產地證明書、重量明細表，包裝明細表，和檢驗證明書等，也視買主國和買賣雙方所定的銷售契約而需要。

中國人： I see. Mr. Brown, will banks accept such documents as presented?

我知道了。伯朗先生，銀行會受理呈交的文件嗎？

外國人： Yes, they will. ***That is***, when shipping documents are required and when no further definition is given, banks can accept them as presented.

** ───

transaction〔træn'sækʃən〕*n.* 業務；處理

definition〔,dɛfə'nɪʃən〕*n.* 限定；定義

會，他們會的。就是說，當需要裝船文件，且又沒有附加的限定時，銀行會受理呈交的文件。

中國人：Thank you very much, Mr. Brown.
謝謝你，伯朗先生。

外國人：You're quite welcome. 別客氣。

Hint Bank—工商人小格言

- To act according to circumstances. 因時制宜。
- Good watch prevents misfortune. 有備無患。
- Where there's a will, there's a way.
  有志者事竟成。
- Man proposes and God disposes.
  謀事在人成事在天。
- To convert defeat into victory.
  反敗爲勝。

4. Shipping Documents 2

裝船文件 2

● **One Point Advice**

其它裝船文件

◇ certificate of origin ⇨ 產地證明書

◇ packing list ⇨ 包裝明細表

◇ inspection certificate ⇨ 檢驗證明書

中國人： Is there any definite interpretation concerning the date of shipment or dispatch of goods?

關於裝船日期或貨物的運送，有明確的說明嗎？

外國人： Yes, of course. The date of the ***Bill of Lading***, or the date of any other document evidencing shipment or dispatch or taking in charge, or the date indicated in the ***reception stamp*** or by notation on any such documents, will be taken in each case to be the date of shipment or dispatch or taking in charge of the goods.

有的，當然有。提單上的日期，或任何載明裝船、運送、收取之其它文件上的日期，收發印鑑上指定的日期，或是任何此類文件備忘錄上，附記的日期，都可視爲裝船、運送或收取的個別日期。

**

interpretation〔ɪn,tɜprɪ'teʃən〕*n.* 說明；解釋

notation〔no'teʃən〕*n.* 備忘錄；附記

中國人： I see. ***Say***, what is the difference between the terms "***freight prepaid***" and "***freight to be prepaid***?"

我懂了。對了，"***freight prepaid***"和"***freight to be prepaid***"有什麼不同？

外國人： Well, ***according to*** the definition, if the words "***freight prepaid***" or "***freight paid***" appear by stamp or some other form on the documents evidencing shipment or dispatch or taking in charge, they will be accepted as evidence of payment of freight.

嗯，根據定義，如果"freight prepaid"或"freight paid"出現在印鑑上，或以其它形式，出現在載明裝船、運送或收取的文件上時，它們表示運費的支付。

外國人： ***On the other hand***, if the words "freight pre-payable" or "freight to be prepaid" or words of similar effect appear by stamp or otherwise on such documents, they will not be accepted as constituting evidence of the payment of freight.

在另一方面，如果"freight pre-payable"或"freight to be prepaid"，或其它類似的字，出現在印鑑或文件上，它們即無法成爲支付運費的憑證。

中國人： Well then, what are ***clean shipping documents***?

那麼，什麼是無瑕疵裝船文件？

** ———

on the other hand 在另一方面　　constitute〔'kastə,tjut〕*v.* 構成

evidence〔'ɛvədəns〕*n.* 憑證

外國人：They are shipping documents which show no superimposed clause or notation which indicates a defective condition of the goods or of the packaging.

它們是表示，沒有附加條款或附記，來表示貨物或包裝有瑕疵的裝船文件。

中國人：Do banks accept shipping documents bearing clauses or notations that show defects in the goods or packaging?

銀行會受理，因貨物或包裝有瑕疵，而附加條款或附記的裝船文件嗎？

外國人：Well, unless the credit expressly states the clauses or notations which may be accepted, banks will refuse shipping documents bearing such clauses.

嗯，除非信用狀上，有明確地載明可受理的條款或附記，否則，銀行將拒絕受理這些有附加條款的裝船文件。

中國人：***Thank you for*** your kind advice. 謝謝你親切的囑附。

外國人：You are welcome. 別客氣。

**

superimpose〔,supərɪm'poz〕*v*. 附加；添加　clause〔klɔz〕*n*. 條款

Hint Bank—工商人小格言

- To shift for oneself. 自力更生。
- Facts are most convincing. 事實勝於雄辯。
- Time is money. 時間就是金錢。

5. Marine Bills of Lading

海運提單

● **One Point Advice**

賣方在貨物裝船後，即可領到租船大副所簽發的**大副收據**（*M/R*），並以此收據向船公司換取**提單**（***bill of lading***），並將提單寄於買方，由買方向船公司換取**提貨單**（***delivery order***），再由買方持提貨單和**輸入許可證**（***import permit***），領取貨物。

外國人：Well, how do you like your new department, Mr. Wang? Keeping busy, I'm sure.

嗯，王先生，還喜歡你的新部門嗎？我想你一定很忙。

中國人：I sure am! ***By the way***, if you have a minute, ***could you please tell me about*** Bills of Lading?

我是很忙！對了，如果你有空，我可以請教你有關海運提單的事嗎？

外國人：All right. But first, I'd like you to understand that Bills of Lading will be rejected if they are issued by ***forwarding agents***, or if issued under and ***subject to*** the conditions of a ***Charter Party*** and/or if they cover shipment by sailing vessels.

**

reject〔rɪˈdʒɛkt〕*v.* 駁回；拒絕　***forwarding agent*** 貨運代理公司
subject to 遵照；倘若　***Charter Party*** 租船契約

好的，但是首先，我要你先了解，貨運代理公司所開的提單，或遵照租船契約條款，所開立的提單，以及用帆船運貨的提單，都將會被駁回。

中國人： I see. But, what about "***Through Bills of Lading***" issued by shipping companies or their agents, or ***Short Form Bills of Lading*** and so on?

我懂了。但關於船運公司或其代理公司所開立的「全程直航提單」和「簡式提單」等等呢？

外國人： Well, they will of course be accepted ***unless otherwise specified in the credit***.

嗯，它們必然會被受理，除非信用狀上列有相反的規定。

外國人： Furthermore, Bills of Lading issued by shipping companies or their agents covering unitized cargoes, such as those on pallets or in containers, will also be accepted unless otherwise specified in the credit.

再者，船運公司或其代理公司所開立，包括如，以運貨托板或容器等單位包裝的貨物提單，也會被受理，除非信用狀上列有相反的規定。

中國人： All right, I understand. Well then, do Bills of Lading need to show evidence that the goods are loaded on board a named vessel or shipped on a named vessel?

好，我了解了。那麼，提單上必須註明，貨物是裝在登記船舶上，或由登記船舶運送嗎？

**

specify〔'spɛsə,faɪ〕*v*. 列舉；指定　　pallet〔'pælɪt〕*n*. 運貨托板

外國人：That's right. That is of course unless it is otherwise specified on the credit.

是的。除非信用狀上列有相反的規定。

中國人：Exactly how can you tell whether goods are ***on board*** or not? ***Please explain to me in detail.***

你如何正確地知道，貨物是否已在船上呢？請詳細地爲我說明。

外國人：All right. Loading on board a named vessel may be evidenced either by a Bill of Lading, or by means of a notation on the Bill of Lading initialed and dated by the carrier or his agent.

好的。貨物是否已裝上登記船舶，可由提單上的裝船指示，或由船公司或代理商在提單上，所簽發的附記日期得知。

中國人：Thank you very much for the explanation.

非常謝謝你的說明。

外國人：***Not at all***. 不客氣。

**

in detail 詳細地　　initial〔ɪˈnɪʃəl〕*v*. 簽姓名的第一個字母

Hint Bank —工商人小格言

- Look before you leap. 三思而後行。
- Man can conquer nature. 人定勝天。
- Walls have ears. 隔牆有耳

6. Other Shipping Documents

其它裝船文件

● **One Point Advice**

出口商在成立出口契約後，必須先向船公司**洽訂船艙**。再將通過**輸出檢查**（***Inspection Certificate***）的出口貨物搬到**保稅地區**（***bonded area***），並且向海關提示**出口申請書**（***Export Permit***），獲得許可證後即完成海關手續。

中國人： Would you tell me in what cases a bank will accept other types of shipping documents?

請你告訴我，在什麼狀況下，銀行會受理其他形式的裝船文件？

外國人： A bank will accept them when they ***bear the carrier's reception stamp or that of his agent***, or when they bear a signature ***purporting*** to be that of the carrier or his agent.

當文件上蓋有運貨人或其代理商的收發印鑑，或意謂相同的簽名時，則銀行會受理。

中國人： What other shipping documents are accepted by the banks? 銀行也受理哪些其它的裝船文件呢？

**

carrier〔ˈkærɪɚ〕*n.* 運貨人　　purport〔pɚˈport〕*v.* 意謂；聲言

外國人：Banks will consider the following documents as acceptable if they bear a reception stamp or signature ***as I have said before***：

如果下列文件蓋有我剛才說過的收發印鑑或簽名，銀行就會受理。

- Railway Bill of Lading 陸運提單
- Railway Consignment Note 陸運託運單
- Inland Waterway Bill of Lading 國內水運提單
- Inland Waterway Consignment Note 國內水運託運單
- Counterfoil Waybill 提貨單存根
- Postal Receipt 郵遞包裹收據
- Certificate of Mailing 郵寄證明書
- Air Mail Receipt 航空郵寄包裹收據
- Air Waybill 空運提貨單
- Air Consignment Note 空運託運單
- Air Receipt 空運收據
- Trucking Company Bill of Lading 卡車貨運提單

or any other similar documents. 或其它類似的文件。

中國人：When a credit ***calls for*** an attestation or certification of weight in the case of transport ***other than*** by sea, will banks accept a weight stamp or declaration of weight superimposed by the carrier on the shipping documents？

** ———

consignment〔kən'saɪnmənt〕*n.* 託運　attestation〔,ætɛs'teʃən〕*n.* 證明書
certification〔,sɝtəfə'keʃən〕*n.* 保證書
declaration〔,dɛklə'reʃən〕*n.* 申報書

在非海運時，當信用狀要求重量的證明或保證書時，銀行會受理，運貨人在裝船文件上，附加重量印鑑或重量申報書嗎？

外國人： Yes, they will accept it unless the credit calls for a separate or independent certificate of weight.

會的，銀行將會受理，除非信用狀上要求個別，或單獨的重量保證書。

中國人： Thank you very much, Mr. Brown. ***It has been most instructive***. 謝謝你，伯朗先生。這對我幫助很大。

外國人： ***Not at all***. 請別在意。

**
---

instructive〔ɪnˈstrʌktɪv〕*adj*. 有益的；教育的

Hint Bank —工商人小格言

- Pride goes before a fall. 驕者必敗。
- Failure is the mother of success.
  失敗爲成功之母。
- Union is strength. 團結力量大。
- As one sows, so shall he reap.
  種瓜得瓜，種豆得豆。

7. Insurance Documents

保險文件

● **One Point Advice**

申請保險的時候，要在**保險申請單**（ ***insurance application*** ）上填入保險目的、船名及航線、保險金額、保險條件、付費貨幣、投保人或被保險人姓名，付上保費（ ***premium*** ）之後，即可領取**保單**（ ***insurance policy*** ）。

中國人：Hello, is this ABC Trading Company?
喂，這裡是ABC貿易公司嗎？

接線生：Yes, this is ABC Trading. ***Who is speaking, please***?
是的，這裡是ABC公司。請問您是哪位？

中國人：This is John Wang of Taipei Taiyo Company. May I speak to Mr. Brotman?
我是台北大耀公司的王約翰。我可以和波特曼先生說話嗎？

接線生：Yes, certainly. Just a moment, please.
當然可以。請稍等一會。

外國人：Hello, Mr. Wang. How are you? 喂，王先生。你好嗎？

中國人：Quite well, thank you. How have you been?
很好，謝謝你。近來可好？

** ———

trading company 貿易公司

外國人： Just fine, thank you. 很好，謝謝你。

中國人： Well, Mr. Brotman, I'd like to know something about insurance documents. ***First of all***, is it necessary to specifically describe them in the credit?

嗯，波特曼先生。我想了解有關保險文件的事。首先，在信用狀中，必需明確地記載出來嗎？

外國人： Yes, you must. That is, insurance documents must be as specified in the credit, and must be properly issued and/or signed by insurance companies or their agents, or by the underwriters.

是的。在信用狀上，必需明確地記載保險文件，而且必需由保險公司、代理商或保險業者簽好章才開出。

中國人： Well then, what about those cover notes issued by brokers? 那麼，那些由保險經紀人所開出的承保單呢？

外國人： They will not be accepted, unless specifically authorized in the credit.

它們不會被受理，除非在信用狀上，有明確地批准。

中國人： ***What about*** the currency expressed in the insurance documents? 保險文件上列出的通貨時價呢？

外國人： Well, ***unless otherwise specified in the credit***, the insurance document must be expressed in the same currency as in the credit.

**

underwriter〔'ʌndɚ,raɪtɚ〕*n.* 保險業者　　broker〔'brokɚ〕*n.* 經紀人
authorize〔'ɔθə,raɪz〕*v.* 批准；許可

嗯，除非信用狀上，有相反的規定，否則，保險文件上的通貨時價要和信用狀一致。

中國人：***Could you please tell me about*** the minimum amount for which insurance must be effected?

你能告訴我，有關保險的最小數量嗎？

外國人：All right. It's the C.I.F. value of the goods concerned. However, when the C.I.F. value of the goods cannot be determined from the documents ***on their face***, the bank will accept as the minimum amount, the amount of the drawing under the credit or the amount of the relative commercial invoice, whichever is the greater.

好的。這是和包括保險費、運費價格有關的貨物。然而，當從文件表面，無法決定包括保險費、運費的價格時，銀行會從所開出信用狀上的最小數量，和相關商業發票上的數量中，挑選較多的數量，予以受理。

中國人：Thanks, ***I'm obliged to you***. 謝謝，非常感激您。

外國人：You are quite welcome. 您眞客氣。

**——————————

determine〔dɪ'tɝmɪn〕*v*. 決定　　***be obliged to*** 感激

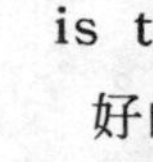

Hint Bank —工商人小格言

❖ Prevention is better than cure. 預防勝於治療。

❖ Practice makes perfect. 熟能生巧。

8. Shipment, Loading or Dispatch

裝船，裝貨或運貨

● One Point Advice

在信用狀上的裝船日期（***dispatch date***）必須寫上明確的期限。如“***prompt shipment***”（迅速裝船）、“***immediate shipment***”（立即裝船）、和“***shipment as soon as possible***”（儘快裝船）之類的用法就**不明確**，且容易引起**誤會**。

中國人：Good morning, Mr. Brotman. How are you this morning?

早安，波特曼先生。今天早上還好嗎？

外國人：Fine thanks, and you? 很好，謝謝，你呢？

中國人：Quite well, thank you. Incidentally, Mr. Brotman, ***I have some questions about*** shipment, loading and dispatch.

非常好，謝謝你。對了，波特曼先生，我對裝船，裝貨和運費，有些問題。

外國人：Yes, of course. What can I do for you?

是的。我能幫你嗎？

中國人：Would you kindly tell me about the definition of the terms such as “shipment,” “loading” and “dispatch” ***in the L/C transactions***?

** ————————

loading〔'lodɪŋ〕*n.* 裝貨

你可否告訴我，在信用狀的業務中，關於「裝船」，「裝貨」和「運貨」的定義？

外國人： Well, unless the terms of the credit indicate otherwise, the words "***departure***," "***dispatch***," "***loading***" or "***sailing***" used in stipulating the latest date for shipment of the goods will be understood ***to be synonymous with*** "shipment."

嗯，除非信用狀上的術語，有其它的規定，否則，用在規定最遲的貨物裝船日期時，這些字如「出發」，「運貨」或「啓航」，都和「裝船」同義。

中國人： I see. May we use such expressions as "prompt shipment," "immediate shipment," "shipment as soon as possible" ***and the like***?

我懂了。我可以使用像「迅速裝船」，「立即裝船」，「儘快裝船」諸如此類的用法嗎？

外國人： Well, ***those expressions are very vague and may cause misunderstandings***. They should not be used.

嗯，這些用法太不明確，且容易引起誤會。你不能使用。

外國人： If they are used, banks will ***interpret*** them ***as*** a request for shipment within thirty days ***from*** the date on the advice of the credit ***to*** the beneficiary by the ***issuing bank*** or by an ***advising bank***, as the case may be.

**

synonymous〔sɪˈnɑnəməs〕*adj.* 同義的；相同的
vague〔veg〕*adj.* 不明確的；含糊的

如果你使用了，銀行將會解釋爲，從開狀銀行或通知銀行，依情況而定，將信用狀通知寄給受益人那天起，請求在三十天以內裝船。

中國人：I understand much better now. 我現在比較了解了。

外國人：Well, Mr. Smith, I'd like to add that the expression "on or about" and similar expressions will be interpreted as a request for shipment during the period from five days before to five days after the specified date, both end days included.

嗯，史密斯先生，我要再說明一點，關於「在或大約」這類的用法，將被解釋爲，請求從指定日期的前五天到後五天內裝船，包括前後兩天在內。

中國人：Thank you so much, Mr. Brotman. It was most instructive. 謝謝你，波特曼先生。這對我幫助很大。

外國人：***Not at all***. 請別客氣。

Hint Bank —工商人小格言

- A prudent man has more than one string to his bow. 有備無患。
- A stitch in time saves nine. 及時行事，事半功倍。
- Rome wasn't built in a day. 羅馬不是一天造成的。
- Well begun, half done. 好的開始是成功的一半。

9. Commercial Invoice

商業發票

● **One Point Advice**

所謂***Commercial Invoice***（**商業發票**），是輸出者寄給輸入者裝運貨物的裝運通知單、物品明細表及價格計算書。對輸入者而言，則是**貨款請求書**。另外，在輸入的時候，被附在**進口報單**（***Import Declaration***）上，當做進口貨物輸入的原賬簿。爲非常重要的貨運單據之一。

中國人：Good morning, Mr. Blake. ***How are you today***?
早安，布萊克先生。今天好嗎？

外國人：Fine thanks, and you? 很好，謝謝，你呢？

中國人：Pretty well, thank you. Mr. Blake, could you please explain to me about the ***commercial invoice***?
非常好，謝謝你。布萊克先生，你能爲我說明，有關商業發票的事嗎？

外國人：All right. The commercial invoice is a bill for the goods ***shipped abroad***. It's not negotiable, and it must show the merchandise that is being sold, the amount to be paid by the buyer, including any charges connected with the shipment, shipment terms such as

** ————————————

commercial invoice 商業發票　negotiable〔nɪ'goʃɪəbl̩〕*adj.* 可轉讓的
merchandise〔'mɝtʃən,daɪz〕*n.* 貨物；商品

F.O.B. or C.I.F., and the marks and numbers on the packages containing the merchandise.
好的。商業發票是將貨物運送至國外的發票。它是不可轉讓的，一張商業發票，必需列有即將出售的貨物名稱，買主應付的款項，包括裝船的費用，如起岸價格或包括保險、運費價格等的裝船條款，和貨物包裝的記號和數量等。

中國人：Is there any other information required on the invoice?
發票上，還需要其它的資料嗎？

外國人：Yes. The date, names and addresses of both the buyer and the seller, the name of the shipping vessel, and ***port of debarkation*** must also be indicated.
是的。必需列出日期，買方和賣方的稱謂和地址，運貨船隻的名稱和上岸的港口。

中國人：I understand much better now. ***By the way***, can banks refuse invoices issued for amounts ***in excess*** of the amount permitted by the credit?
我現在比較了解了。對了，銀行會拒絕，超出信用狀允許數量的超額發票嗎？

外國人：Yes, they can. And unless otherwise specified in the credit, the commercial invoice must be made out ***in the name of*** the applicant for the credit.
會的。而且除非信用狀上，有相反的規定，否則商業發票，必需以信用狀申請人的名義開出。

**

debarkation〔,dibɑr'keʃən〕*n.* 上岸；登陸
excess〔ɪk'sɛs〕*n.* 超過的量或額

中國人：***What about the description of the merchandise in the commercial invoice?***

商業發票上的貨物規格說明書呢？

外國人：Well, it must ***correspond*** exactly ***to*** the description in the credit. ***It is preferable***, however, ***that*** merchandise descriptions in all documents ***correspond*** exactly ***to*** the description in the credit.

嗯，它必需和信用狀上的規格說明書完全符合。然而，最好所有文件上的規格說明書，都和信用狀上的說明書完全符合。

中國人：I see. Thank you very much indeed.

我懂了。眞的非常感謝你。

外國人：You're quite welcome. ***Please call again if you have any questions.***

不用客氣。如果還有別的問題，請再打電話給我。

**

correspond〔,kɔrə'spɑnd〕*v.* 符合

Hint Bank — 工商人小格言

- Don't count your chickens before they hatch.
  不要打如意算盤。
- Little drops of water make the mighty ocean.
  積少成多。
- Strike while the iron is hot. 打鐵趁熱。

10. Negotiating a Documentary Bill of Exchange

押滙作業

● **One Point Advice**

銀行的押滙程序：

①銀行根據信用狀的條款，將運貨人提呈的裝船文件**押滙**，以當天的滙率報價，付給**受益人**（***beneficiary***）貨價。

②銀行將**裝船文件**送至開狀銀行或議付銀行。

③從**開狀銀行**（***opening bank***）或**議付銀行**（***reimbursing bank***），收到滙票的貨價。

中國人：I'd like to know the bank's procedure for an ***export transaction*** under a letter of credit.

我想了解一下，有關銀行對信用狀的出口業務程序。

外國人：All right. Let me explain the procedure for the ***negotiation of an export bill*** on a US dollar basis with an L/C, which is the most common in ordinary export transactions.

好的。讓我爲你說明一下，以美元開出信用狀的押滙程序，這是一般出口業務中，最普遍的一種。

外國人：We（＝*banks*）negotiate the shipping documents presented by the shipper according to the L/C terms

---

** ***bill of exchange*** 滙票

and pay the beneficiary the proceeds at the exchange rate quoted on that date.

我們（銀行）根據信用狀的條款，將運貨人提呈的裝船文件押滙，以當天的滙率報價，付給受益人貨價。

外國人：We forward the shipping documents to the appropriate bank, usually the L/C opening bank, the reimbursing bank, and any others mentioned in the terms of the L/C.

我們將裝船文件送至適當的銀行，通常是開狀銀行，議付銀行和信用狀上提到的其它銀行。

外國人：We receive the proceeds of the exchange bill from the L/C opening bank or reimbursing bank.

我們從開狀銀行或議付銀行；收到滙票的貨價。

外國人：The reimbursing method is usually mentioned in the L/C under "special instructions."

在信用狀上，通常對付款的方式有「特別規定」。

外國人：This is a rough explanation of export negotiations ***from the viewpoint of*** the bank.

這是從銀行的觀點，對出口押滙而作的簡要說明。

中國人：Thank you very much. I think I understand the rough scheme of export transactions with an L/C.

非常謝謝你。我想我對出口押滙的架構，有初步的了解了。

**

proceeds〔prəʹsidz〕*n.pl.* 銷售額；收益　***reimbursing bank*** 議付銀行
scheme〔skim〕*n.* 架構

中國人：Are there any special points we have ***to be careful about*** in these transactions?

在這些業務中，還有需要特別注意的事嗎？

外國人：Yes, there are. First of all, you should ***make sure*** that the required number of shipping documents are presented and the contents of the documents presented must be carefully ***checked against*** the L/C before paying the proceeds to the shipper.

是的。首先，在付給運貨人貨價以前，你必須檢查裝船文件的數目、內容，以確定是否與信用狀符合。

中國人：I see. Is that what is called a "document check?"

我懂了。這是不是稱爲「文件檢查」？

外國人：That's right. ***At the same time***, you have to see about any stipulated "special instructions," including the reimbursing method by carefully examining the L/C.

是的。同時，你必需仔細檢視信用狀，注意任何規定的特別指示，包括付款的方式。

外國人：Should you misunderstand the method of reimbursement, this could result in a delay in our receiving the proceeds or make an "unpaid" claim action necessary.

萬一你誤解了議付的方式，將會造成我們收取貨價的延遲，並且，使我們必需發出「貨價未付」的聲明。

**

first of all 首先　　reimbursement〔,riɪm'bɝsmənt〕*n.* 償付

外國人： ***In any case***, you should try to check all the documents against the relevant L/C. You will, then, come to handle necessary procedures correctly ***step by step***.

無論如何，你應該檢查所有的文件，是否和有關的信用狀符合。然後，再逐步地進行必需的程序。

中國人： Thank you very much for the explanation. ***In short***, you mean, " ***practice makes perfect*** " and " ***experience is the best teacher.*** " ***I will try my best.***

非常謝謝你的說明。簡單地說，你的意思是「熟能生巧」和「經驗是最好的老師。」我會盡力的。

**

relevant 〔'rɛləvənt〕 *adj.* 有關的；切題的　　***in short*** 簡單地說

Hint Bank — 工商人小格言

- First come, first served. 先下手爲強。
- Actions speak louder than words. 行動勝於空談。
- All good things come to an end.
  天下無不散之筵席。
- Bad news travels fast. 壞事傳千里。
- Least said, soonest mended. 禍從口出。

11. Presentation & Date Terms

呈交與日期的專門用語

● **One Point Advice**

L/C（信用狀）的**有效日期**（*expiry date*）是從*L/C*開出日起至押滙銀行押滙爲止。***L/C*統一慣例**規定，須寫明裝船期限、有效期限，以及完成裝船到押滙的期限。

中國人：Excuse me, Mr. Brotman. Would you kindly tell me about ***the presentation of documents*** in the L/C transactions?

對不起，波特曼先生。你可否告訴我，有關信用狀業務中，文件的呈交事宜？

外國人：Yes, certainly. At first, ***according to*** the requirement of Article 37 of the UCPDC, every credit must stipulate ***an expiry date*** for presentation of documents.

當然可以。首先，根據憑單據付信用狀統一慣例，第三十七條規定，每份信用狀必需訂明呈交文件的有效日期。

外國人：The credits must also stipulate a specified period of time after the date of issuance of the Bills of Lading or other shipping documents ***during which*** presentation

** ————————————

according to 根據　requirement〔rɪ'kwaɪrmənt〕*n.* 規定；要求
issuance〔'ɪʃuəns, 'ɪʃju-〕*n.* 開立；發行

of documents for payment, acceptance or negotiation must be made.

信用狀上,也必需在提單或其它文件開立後,規定一段期限,在這段期限中,要呈交付款,承兌或押滙的文件。

中國人: I see. If no such period of time is stipulated in the credit, how do banks handle the documents presented?

我懂了。如果信用狀上,沒有規定這個期限,銀行將如何處理呈交的文件?

外國人: Well, banks will refuse documents presented to them later than 21 days after the date of issuance of the Bills of Lading or other shipping documents.

嗯,銀行會拒絕受理在開出提單或其它裝船文件後的二十一天,才呈交的文件。

外國人: Furthermore, banks are ***under no obligation to*** accept presentation of documents ***outside their banking hours***.

再者,銀行沒有義務,在非營業時間內,受理呈交的文件。

中國人: Well, would you tell me about ***Date Terms***, such as the "first half," or the "second half" of a month? Can we use these terms?

嗯,你可否告訴我,有關日期的專門用語,像一個月的「前半」或「後半」之類的?我們可以使用這些用法嗎?

** ──────────

negotiation〔nɪ,goʃɪ′eʃən〕*n.* 押滙;(票據的)流通

obligation〔,ɑblə′geʃən〕*n.* 義務;責任

外國人：Yes, we can. They are ***interpreted***, respectively, ***as*** from the lst to the 15th, and the 16th to the last day of each month, inclusive.

是的，可以使用。它們分別代表，每個月的一號到十五號，和十六號到最後一號，包括前後兩天在內。

中國人：I see. How about the interpretation of the terms "***beginning***," "***middle***," or "***end***" of a month?

我懂了。關於「月初」，「月中」或「月末」這類的用法呢？

外國人：Well, they are interpreted to mean, respectively, as from the lst to the 10th, the 11th to the 20th, and the 21st to the last day of each month, inclusive.

嗯，它們分別代表，每個月的一號到十號，十一號到二十號，和二十一號到最後一號，包括前後兩天在內。

中國人：Thank you very much for your help. 非常謝謝你的幫忙。

外國人：You're welcome. 請別客氣。

**

respectively〔rɪ'spɛktɪvlɪ〕*adv*. 分別地；個別地

Hint Bank —工商人小格言

- Security is the greatest enemy. 生於憂患死於安樂。
- Wise men learn by other men's mistakes.
  智者從他人的錯誤中學習。
- Better late than never. 只要開始，雖晚不遲。

12. Foreign Exchange Rate

匯率

● One Point Advice

◇ ***T.T.S. rate*** ⇨ ***Telegraphic Transfer Selling rate*** **電匯賣出匯率**爲銀行賣出外幣給顧客時，所報的滙率。

◇ ***T.T.B. rate*** ⇨ ***Telegraphic Transfer Buying rate*.** **電滙買進滙率**爲銀行買進外幣時，所報的滙率。

顧　客：Hello. How are you? 嗨。你好嗎？

出納員：Fine thanks, and you? 好，謝謝，你呢？

顧　客：Very well, I was recently transferred to our international department from the textile department. My new job is in exports and imports. However, ***this kind of business is completely new to me***, so I was wondering if you could tell me about foreign exchange rates.

很好，我最近剛從紡織部門，調到國際部門。我負責進出口的業務。然而，我對這類業務完全陌生，所以我在想，你是否能告訴我，有關外滙滙率的事。

出納員：All right. Roughly speaking the exchange rate can be divided into two kinds, when the bank sells foreign

**

transfer〔 træns′fɝ 〕 *v*. 調職；轉任

textile〔′tɛkstl̩ ,-taɪl 〕 *adj*. 紡織的　　divide〔 dɪ′vaɪd 〕 *v*. 分開

currency to customers and when the bank buys foreign currency from them. Please note that the words "selling rate" and "buying rate" are ***from the bank's point of view.***

好的。大致說來，滙率可分為兩種，當銀行賣出外幣給顧客，和向顧客買進外幣。請注意，「賣出滙率」和「買進滙率」是從銀行的觀點而言。

顧　客：I have heard something about a T.T.S. rate and a T.T.B. rate. Please explain what these terms actually mean.

我曾經聽過T.T.S.滙率和T.T.B.滙率。論解釋這兩個名詞的正確意義。

出納員：Certainly. "T.T.S. rate" means the Telegraphic Transfer Selling rate, which is the rate quoted in case the bank sells foreign currency to a customer, ***and it's the other way round for "T.T.B. rate"***, the Telegraphic Transfer Buying rate.

當然好。「T.T.S.滙率」是指電滙賣出滙率，是當銀行賣出外幣給顧客時，所報的滙率，和它相反的是「T.T.B.滙率」，電滙買進滙率。

顧　客：I see. Now please tell me, if you would, how you quote the rate in the negotiation of export bills?

我懂了。現在是否能請你告訴我，在兌換出口滙票時，你們是如何報出滙率？

**

foreign currency 外幣

出納員： OK. We have an "***at sight rate***" and a "***usance rate***." The "at sight rate" is quoted ***taking into consideration*** the number of mailing days for the negotiated shipping documents to be received by the bank which opened the L/C.

好的。我們有「見票滙率」和「遠期支票滙率」兩種。「見票滙率」是考慮押滙裝船，文件郵寄到開狀銀行所需的日數。

出納員： Now, the bank will quote a "usance rate" ***in consideration of*** the time it takes (us) to receive the proceeds.

現在，銀行報出「遠期支票滙率」，即是將(我們)收到貨價的時間列入考慮。

出納員： ***In other words***, the bank deducts a "usance interest" from the T.T.B. rate at the time of negotiation of export bills.

換句話說，銀行在押滙出口滙票時，即從電傳買進滙率中扣除「遠期支票利息」。

顧　客： I think I understand. Then the term "acceptance rate" which is used for imports is the opposite of the "at sight rate" for exports. Am I correct?

我想我了解了。那麼，用於進口的「承兌滙率」和用於出口的「見票滙率」剛好相反。我說得對嗎？

出納員： Yes, ***you've got it***. 是的，你說對了。

** ———

export bill 出口滙票　usance〔 'juzəns 〕*n*. 支付滙票的習慣期限
deduct〔 dɪ'dʌkt 〕*v*. 扣除

顧　客：But, this is really quite complicated, don't you agree?
但是，這確實有些複雜，你同意嗎？

出納員：Sure, but you will ***get accustomed to*** this terminology through coming ***in contact with*** it in your daily trading business.
當然，但是，經由你日常業務的接觸之後，你會習慣這些專門用語的。

** ———

get accustomed to 習慣　terminology〔,tɜmə'nɑlədʒɪ〕*n.* 專門用語
contact〔'kɑntækt〕*n.* 接觸

Hint Bank—工商人小格言

- Comparisons are odious. 人比人氣死人。
- A contented mind is a perpetual feast. 知足常樂。
- Don't change horses in mid-stream. 臨陣勿換將。
- You cannot sell the cow and drink the milk.
  魚與熊掌不可兼得。
- Still water runs deep. 靜水流深。
- Two heads are better than one. 集思廣益。

附錄

貿易常用語彙

● 一般業務用語

accounts payable	應付帳目
accounts receivable	應收帳目
advertiser ['ædvɚ,taɪzɚ] *n.*	廣告主
advertising ['ædvɚ,taɪzɪŋ] *n.*	廣告業
agent ['edʒənt] *n.*	代理商
allowance [ə'laʊəns] *n.*	特別經費
annual office outing	公司年度運動會
annual rate	年率
annual report	年度報告
arbitrator ['ɑrbə,tretɚ] *n.*	仲裁者
A.S.A.P. (= *As Soon As Possible*)	越快越好
assumption [ə'sʌmpʃən] *n.*	假設
automated office	自動化設備辦公室
bad debt	呆帳
bail out	企業救濟
balance of contract	未履行契約
ban [bæn] *n.*	禁止
banking ['bæŋkɪŋ] *n.*	銀行業務
bank rate (discount rate)	銀行所定的貼現率(利率)
bankruptcy ['bæŋkrʌptsɪ] *n.*	破產
bearish ['bɛrɪʃ] *adj.*	(股票)下跌的
belt tightening	採取緊縮政策

blue sky laws	禁止財務不健全的公司推銷其股票的法律
board of directors	董事會
bottom out	降到底線
boost [bust] *n.*	增加
bolster [ˈbolstɚ] *v.*	支持
bn (= *billion*)	十億之簡稱
breakthrough [ˈbrek,θru] *n.*	突破
budget [ˈbʌdʒɪt] *n.*	預算
bullish [ˈbʊlɪʃ] *adj.*	行情看漲的
B.S. (= *Business School*)	商業學校之簡稱
business ethics	商業道德
bust [bʌst] *n.*	破產
buy off	收買
claim [klem] *n.*	賠償損害要求
commodity [kəˈmɑdətɪ] *n.*	商品
compensation [,kɑmpənˈseʃən] *n.*	賠償金
consignee [,kɑnsaɪˈni] *n.*	收件人
consortium [kənˈsɔrʃɪəm] *n.*	國際財團
consumer durable	耐久消費財
consumer goods	消費財
convention [kənˈvɛnʃən] *n.*	集會
counter offer	還價
counter purchase	互惠交換採購
coupon clipper	(專以剪兌公債之利息票爲事的)富人

crude oil	原油
curb [kɝb] *v.*	抑制
cutback ['kʌt,bæk] *n.*	削減
decision maker	決策者
deficit ['dɛfəsɪt] *n.*	赤字
demography [dɪ'mɑgrəfɪ] *n.*	人口統計
depress [dɪ'prɛs] *v.*	蕭條
dismantle [dɪs'mæntḷ] *v.*	撤銷
dividends ['dɪvə,dɛndz] *n.*	股息
dog days	經濟停滯期
dog's life	潦倒的生活
domestic economy	國內經濟
downturn ['daʊntɝn] *n.*	不景氣
economic aid	經濟援助
economic growth	經濟成長
economic growth rate	經濟成長率
economic recession	經濟蕭條
energy crisis	能源危機
estimate ['ɛstə,met] *v.*	估計
exchange market	交易市場
expense accounts	經費帳目
expiry date	期滿日期
fair market value	公正市場價格
federal express	聯邦快遞公司
feedstock ['fid,stɑk] *n.*	機械原料
files [faɪlz] *n. pl.*	檔案

final offer	最終提案
firm offer	確認訂單
fiscal year	會計年度
flextime [ˈfleks,taɪm] *n.*	彈性工作時間
float [flot] *n.*	發行（公債）
fluke [fluk] *n.*	僥倖
formula [ˈfɔrmjələ] *n.*	公式；規格
fortune 500	美國財星雜誌票選之五百大企業
full employment	全職雇用
G.A.A.P. (= *Generally Accepted Accounting Principles*)	一般會計原則
general account	一般會計
goodwill [ˈgʊdˈwɪl] *n.*	商譽；信譽
glut [glʌt] *v.*	供應過多
greenback [ˈgrin,bæk] *n.*	美鈔
headhunter [ˈhɛd,hʌntɚ] *n.*	求才者
incentive program	激勵計劃
indent [ɪnˈdɛnt] *n.*	委託採購
insolvent [ɪnˈsɑlvənt] *adj.*	無力償付債務的
institutional investor	機構投資者
intervention [,ɪntɚˈvɛnʃən] *n.*	干涉
inventory adjustment	存貨調整
investment [ɪnˈvɛstmənt] *n.*	投資
jawbone [ˈdʒɔˈbon, -,bon] *n.*	施以强大壓力的說服方式
job interview	求職面試
kickback [ˈkɪk,bæk] *n.*	回扣

killing ['kılıŋ] ***n.***	（股票投機）大發利市
kiss-off ['kıs,ɔf, -,ɑf] ***n.***	解雇
leading indicator	景氣先行指標
legend ['lɛdʒənd] ***n.***	長期受歡迎的商品
loss leader	爲招徠顧客虧本賣出之廉價品
massive ['mæsıv] ***adj.***	巨額的
mega- ['mɛgə-] ***n.***	表示100萬的接頭語
mergers and acquisitions	吸收合併
minute book	會議記錄
missionary selling	宣傳普及推銷
money supply	通貨供給量
monopoly [mə'nɑpḷı] ***n.***	壟斷；獨佔
moratorium [,mɔrə'torıəm] ***n.***	延期償付
mortgage ['mɔrgıdʒ] ***n.***	抵押
multinational [,mʌltı'næʃənḷ] ***adj.***	多國的
negative growth	負成長
negative interest	負利息
negative list	限制輸入品的名單
non-tariff barrier	非關稅壁壘
NOPEC	OPEC加盟國以外的石油輸出國
obscene profit	總獲利
old boy network	求過於供之市場狀況
oligopoly [,ɑlə'gɑpəlı] ***n.***	寡占
organizational structure	組織構造
pay off	分紅
per capita income	每人的收入

perks [pɝks] *n.*	臨時收入
personal consumption	個人消費
physical labor	肉體勞動
policy and procedure manual	政策手續手册
prime rate	最優惠利率
profit ['prɑfɪt] *n.*	利益
profiteer [,prɑfə'tɪr] *n.*	獲暴利者
program ['progræm] *n.*	計劃；預定表
promotion [prə'moʃən] *n.*	昇遷
property tax	固定財產稅
prospectus [prə'spɛktəs, prɑ-] *n.*	發起書
protectionism [prə'tɛkʃənɪzm̩] *n.*	貿易保護主義
public fares	公共費用
purchasing power	購買力
qualitative ['kwɑlə,tetɪv] *adj.*	質的
quantitative ['kwɑntə,tetɪv] *adj.*	量的
quality ['kwɑlətɪ] *n.*	品質
quantity ['kwɑntətɪ] *n.*	數量
quarter ['kwɔrtɚ] *n.*	季（三個月）
quota ['kwotə] *n.*	配額
rat race	公司職員的升遷競爭
red eye	飛機的夜行班次
regulation [,rɛgjə'leʃən] *n.*	規定
reimbursement [,riɪm'bɝsmənt] *n.*	退款；償還
reindustrialization [rɪɪn,dʌstrɪələ-'zeʃən, -aɪ'ze-] *n.*	再工業化

release [rɪ'lis] *v.*	發表
retaliation [rɪ,tælɪ'eʃən] *n.*	報復
saudi soda	石油
seasonal adjustment	季節調整
security [sɪ'kjʊrətɪ] *n.*	保障
seniority [sin'jɔrətɪ] *n.*	年資；資歷
shark [ʃɑrk] *n.*	放高利者
short list	有資格投標人名單
short selling	賣空
sick day	生病請假
spot check	抽樣調查
statistics [stə'tɪstɪks] *n.*	統計
sterling ['stɝlɪŋ] *n.*	英國貨幣
stockpile ['stɑk,paɪl] *n.*	儲備
strategy ['strætədʒɪ] *n.*	戰略
streamline ['strim,laɪn] *v.*	使簡化
structurally depressed	構造不佳
subsidy ['sʌbsədɪ] *n.*	津貼
suggestion box	意見箱
sunrise industry	新興產業
superior [sə'pɪrɪɚ, sʊ-] *n.*	上司
supply and demand	供需關係
sustain [sə'sten] *v.*	維持
synergy ['sɪnɚdʒɪ] *n.*	共同作用
telemarketing ['tɛlə,mɑrkɪtɪŋ] *n.*	透過電視螢幕來購物
tender ['tɛndɚ] *v.*	招標

territory 〔'tɛrə,torɪ〕*n.* 銷售區域
time management 時間管理
training session 訓練階段
transfer 〔træns'fɝ〕*v.* 調職
two-career family 兩夫婦皆上班的家庭
universal product code 統一商品密碼
upstream 〔'ʌp'strim〕*n.* 上流社會
vend 〔vɛnd〕*v.* 販賣
wash out 解除契約
windfall profits 意外收穫
working breakfast 早餐會報
XYZ（= *Examine Your Zipper*） 請注意你的拉鍊
zillionaire 〔,zɪljən'ɛr〕*n.* 擁有無數財產的人

● **貨物運輸用語**

abandon 〔ə'bændən〕*v.* 遺棄（貨物）
act of God 天災；不可抗力
address commission 基於租船契約給予運費打折
average 〔'ævərɪdʒ〕*n.* 海損
ballast 〔'bæləst〕*n.* 壓艙物
bill of lading 海運提單
bulk 〔'bʌlk〕*n.* 散裝貨
bunker 〔'bʌŋkɚ〕*n.* （船上的）煤倉
clean B/L 無瑕疵提單
charter party 租船契約
combination carrier 可兼運固體和液體貨物的船

congestion [kən'dʒɛstʃən] *n.*	港口擁擠
container ship	貨櫃船
dead freight	船艙未裝滿仍需付的運費
demurrage [dɪ'mɝɪdʒ] *n.*	延期停泊費
detention charge	扣押貨物費
differential tariff	差額關稅
discretion [dɪ'skrɛʃən] *n.*	自由判斷
dispute [dɪ'spjut] *n.*	紛爭
embargo [ɪm'bɑrgo] *n.*	禁運；禁止通商
evaluation [ɪ,væljʊ'eʃən] *n.*	評價
expected time of departure	預定出港日期
full container load	貨櫃裝貨量
freight [fret] *n.*	貨物；運費
fully containerized ship	貨櫃專用船
geared ship	有起重機裝備能自行裝卸貨的船
hold [hold] *n.*	普通船裏的船倉
inland transportation	內陸運輸
insurance policy	保險單
intermodal transportation	海陸運輸
shipping documents	裝船文件
stale B/L	逾期提單
stem [stɛm] *n.*	船首
stevedore ['stivə,dor,-,dɔr] *n.*	碼頭工人
stowed and trimmed	貨物裝船和散裝貨打包
transship [træns'ʃɪp] *v.*	換船
van [væn] *n.*	貨櫃

CHAPTER 4

琳琅滿目話商展

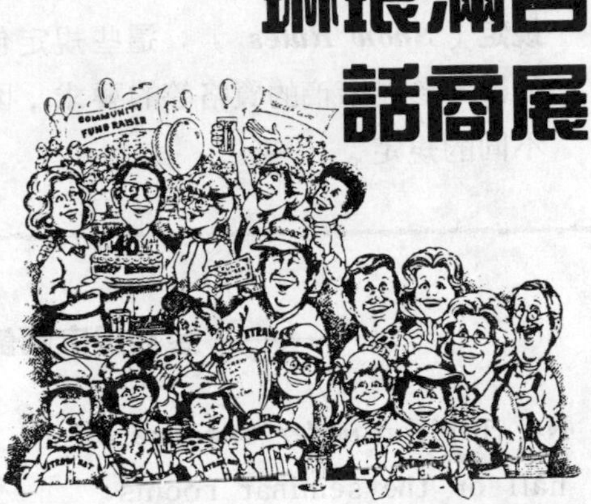

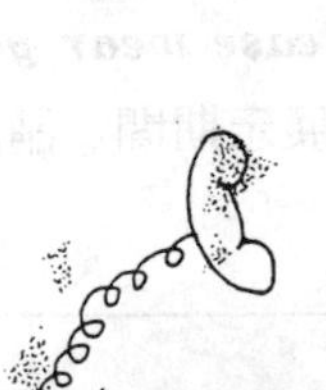

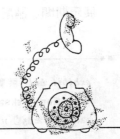

1 General Information for a Fair
策劃商展須知

《 *Welcome Letter* 》

收到國外寄來的參展邀請函時，首先必須對整份文件，加以細看，明白其中的細節及所提供的資訊。另外必須注意**參展規定**（***Show Rules***）：這些規定包括對舉辦的日期、會場的佈置、參展廠商的資格等的要求，因此會因為商展的性質而有不同的規定。

參展規定關鍵句

♤ No children ***under the age of*** 18 are allowed in the exhibit hall or the seminar rooms.
未滿十八歲的兒童，不准進入會場及研討室中。

♤ Badges must be worn to all official conference and exhibition activities. 出席正式會議及展覽活動，請配帶名牌。

♤ ***Please wear your badge at all times.***
展示期間，請配帶名牌。

**

exhibit hall 展覽會場　　seminar〔,sɛmə'nɑr〕*n.* 研討會
exhibition〔,ɛksə'bɪʃə〕*n.* 展覽會
badge〔bædʒ〕*n.*（表示身分、職位的）證章；名牌

♧ No banners, signs, flags or placards may be displayed or distributed in aisles.
走道上，不准懸掛或散發標幟，招牌，旗子或招貼等物品。

♧ No cameras or other photographic equipment may be brought into the convention ***without the permission of show management***. 未經主辦單位允許，不得將相機或其它攝影器材帶入會場。

♧ Violators of these rules will be removed from the convention. 違反規定者，將被撤離出會場。

♧ Shopping bags are allowed. 可以攜帶購物袋入場。

♧ Spouses accompanying qualified registrants are admitted free. 合格登記者之配偶可免費入場。

♧ No one under the age of 18 will be admitted to the exhibition. 未滿十八歲不得進入會場。

** ─────────────

banner〔'bænɚ〕*n*. 旗幟；標幟　placard〔'plækard〕*n*. 布告；招貼
distribute〔dɪ'strɪbjʊt〕*v*. 分發；散發　aisle〔aɪl〕*n*. 走道
convention〔kən'vɛnʃən〕*n*. 會場；大會　remove〔rɪ'muv〕*v*. 移開
spouse〔spaʊz〕*n*. 配偶　exhibition〔ˌɛksə'bɪʃən〕*n*. 展覽會

2 Decorating the Booth
佈置會場實用語

《 ***Proper order*** 》

一般的國際商展，皆會提供展示**攤位**（***booth***），但要如何佈置展示空間，則爲參展廠商自行負責。因此從訂製櫃台、展示架到海報、圖表懸掛招牌，都得用英語和當地的佈置人員溝通。如果你發現展示的產品，放置不當時，請說：***Please move these three computer display shelves a little more to the left***，***OK***？（請將這三台電腦展示架，移到左邊好嗎？）

交待會場工作人員

♤ Please nail two rectangular display shelves here.
請在這裡，釘二個長方形的展示架。

♤ Please ***nail up*** a sign board above the counter and paint our company's name on it.
請在櫃台的上方，釘上一面招牌，並漆上我們公司的名稱。

♤ Please help us ***put up*** a triangular activity sign board ***in the doorway***.
請幫我們在門口，豎立一個三角形的活動看板。

**

display shelf 展示架　　signboard〔'saɪn,bɔrd〕*n*. 招牌；看板

♤ Please hang this map on the right-hand wall.
請將這幅地圖，懸掛在右面的牆上。

♤ Please move these three computer display shelves ***a little more to the left***, OK？
請將這三台電腦展示架，移到左邊好嗎？

♤ Would you please change this picture？
請把這幅照片換下來，好嗎？

♤ Please install ten colored light bulbs for us.
請爲我們裝置十串彩色燈泡。

♤ Would you please help us carry this machine into the hall？
請幫忙我們將這台機器搬進場內，好嗎？

♤ We need ten chairs and three long tables.
我們需要十張椅子和三張長桌。

♤ Please ***divide*** this room ***into*** two booths by using a wooden screen. 請你用隔板，把這裡隔爲二間展示攤。

♤ Please put a round counter with high legs in the middle of the booth. 麻煩你在攤位中間，放置一個高脚圓形的櫃台。

♤ We'll order a glass display counter.
我們要訂製一個玻璃展示櫃。

** ———

install〔ɪn'stɔl〕*v*. 裝置　bulb〔bʌlb〕***n***. 燈泡
divide〔dɪ'vaɪd〕*v*. 隔開　screen〔skrin〕***n***. 隔板

♤ We'll ***set up*** an outdoor canopy right here.
我們在這裡要搭一個露天篷子。

佈置攤位

♤ Please ***paste up*** these posters on the walls in the surrounding hallways. 請你將這些海報，貼在會場的四周。

♤ These are catalogues and pamphlets of our company's products, please put them on the left side of the counter.
這些是我們公司的產品目錄和傳單，請將他們放在櫃台的左側。

♤ We need a vase of flowers, and a tea set on the display shelf. 展示架上，需要一盆花來裝飾，另外還要一組茶具。

♤ Please make a POP poster for our new products.
請製作一張宣傳新產品的 POP 海報。

♤ ***Remember to give our buyers your smiling face.***
客戶參觀時，要記得面帶微笑。

♤ Please sort these products and ***write down their brands on sheets of card-board.***
請把這些產品，做好歸類，並在硬紙板上，寫下品牌名稱。

♤ Please place this big model doll ***in front of*** the entrance.
將這個大模型娃娃放在入口處。

** ———

paste〔pest〕*v.* 張貼　　catalogue〔ˈkætə,lɔg〕*n.* 目錄
pamphlet〔ˈpæmflɪt〕*n.* 傳單；小冊子

♤ Please ***hand out*** these balloons to the children who come to the product show. 請把這些汽球，分送給參觀的兒童們。

♤ Please stick a piece of paper saying "No Touch" on this glass counter. 請在這個玻璃櫃上，貼上一張「請勿觸摸」的條子。

♤ Let buyers leave their telephone numbers and addresses on this notebook. 記得請客戶在筆記簿上，留下聯絡的電話和地址。

改變展示的攤位

♤ We can't find our booth in the hall ; our number is booth 102. 我們在場中，找不到我們公司的攤位，號碼是102。

♤ Could we ***exchange*** booths ***with*** the company in the corner ? We need this corner to display our products.
我們可否要求和轉角的公司，交換攤位？我們需要一個轉角處來展示產品。

♤ Could you please remove this signboard to the left side ? Then it won't stand ***in the way*** of our entrance.
可否請你們將這個看板移向左邊？這樣才不會擋住我們的入口處。

** ———

balloon〔bə'lun〕*n.* 氣球　　stick〔stɪk〕*v.* 黏貼
exchange〔ɪks'tʃendʒ〕*v.* 交換　　***in the way*** 防礙；擋路

Introducing the Products
接待展示實用語

《 ***May I help you?*** 》

一切佈置就緒之後，就等**客戶**（***buyer***）上門了。首先，你必須記得要面帶**微笑**，主動詢問客戶：***May I help you***?（需要我幫忙嗎？），並且將準備好的傳單、手冊附贈給客戶做參考。如果客戶欲立即訂購時，需事先準備好一切的文件，千萬不要手忙脚亂，給客戶留下不好的印象。

招呼用語

♤ ***May I help you***? 需要我幫忙嗎？

♤ Let me introduce this to you. 讓我爲您介紹。

♤ Good morning, sir. May I help you?
先生，早安。我能爲您效勞嗎？

♤ ***Please take your time***. 請慢慢看。

♤ What can I do for you? 我能爲您作些什麼嗎？

推薦新產品

♤ This is our newly developed product. ***Would you like to see it***? 這是我們最新開發成功的產品。您要不要看一看？

♤ You must ***be interested in*** seeing our new product.
您一定有興趣看看我們的新產品。

♤ ***This product is the result of our latest technology.***
這項產品是我們最新技術的成果。

♤ I'm sure you'll ***be satisfied with*** this new product.
我相信您一定會對這項新產品十分滿意。

介紹暢銷產品

♤ This product ***sells well*** in Europe. 這項產品在歐洲非常暢銷。

♤ There is a great demand for this product.
這項產品的需求量很大。

♤ ***I'm convinced that*** this product will sell well.
我有把握，這項產品一定會很暢銷。

示範操作

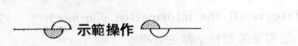

♤ ***Let me show you*** how to operate this machine.
讓我爲您示範這部機器的操作方式。

♤ If you fold this ball-point pen, it becomes a key ring.
將這枝原子筆對折一次，它就變成一把鑰匙圈。

**

technology〔tɛk'nɑlədʒɪ〕*n.* 技術　　satisfy〔'sætɪs,faɪ〕*n.* 使滿意
convince〔kən'vɪns〕*v.* 使信服　　fold〔fold〕*v.* 對折
key ring 鑰匙圈

♤ If you press the belly of this toy doll, it will sing a song.
在這個玩具娃娃的肚子按一下，它就會唱歌。

♤ The locket of this pearl necklace can be opened and you can put a photo on it. 這串珍珠項鍊的墜子，可以打開，並裝上照片。

♤ The sleaves of this coat can be ***taken off***. So, it is suitable for both summer and winter.
這件外衣，可以將袖子拆下來。因此多夏皆宜。

附贈傳單、目錄

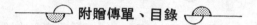

♤ This is the catalogue of our products.
這是本公司產品的目錄。

♤ Please take this information ***for your reference***.
這些資料送給您作參考。

♤ Here is all the information you need.
您需要的資料，都在這裡。

價格折扣問題

♤ If you place a large-scale order, we have a discount for you. 如果您願意大批訂購，我們將有特別優待。

♤ During the display period, ***all our products have a ten percent discount***. 展示期間，我們的產品一律打九折。

**

belly〔'bɛlɪ〕*n*. 肚子　locket〔'lɑkɪt〕*n*. 懸於項鍊下的小盒
reference〔'rɛfərəns〕*n*. 參考　large-scale〔'lɑrdʒ'skel〕*adj*. 大規模的

♤ If you order ten thousand pieces, we may consider giving you a twenty five percent discount.
如果您訂購一萬件，我們可以考慮打七五折。

♤ This is our ***bottom price***, so we can't give you any discount.
這是我們的底價，所以無法再打折了。

♤ Our price is much lower than the current market price.
這已經比市價便宜很多了。

♤ If you add a little more again, then we can ***make a deal***.
如果您再加一些，我們就成交。

交換名片和聯絡地址

♤ Here is my name card. 這是我的名片。

♤ This is our company's address and telephone number. If you have any questions, ***don't hesitate to contact us***.
這是我們公司的聯絡地址和電話。有任何問題，請不要客氣，馬上與我們聯絡。

♤ Please leave your address and telephone number for service after the sale.
請您留下您的聯絡地址和電話，以便日後爲您提供售後服務。

**

bottom price 底價　***make a deal*** 成交
contact〔'kɑntækt〕*v.* 聯絡

♤ We'll mail our latest catalogue to you.
我們將寄上本公司最新的產品目錄給您。

♤ These are telephone numbers and addresses of our branch offices in the U.S. You are welcome to contact them.
這是我們全美分公司的電話及地址。歡迎您來洽詢。

處理立即訂購事宜

♤ Please ***write down*** your name and the products you want to order on this order sheet.
請在這份訂單上塡寫您的大名，和訂購的產品。

♤ We'll advise you about the details concerning payment and delivery of goods by FAX.
我們將以傳眞通知您，有關付款交貨的詳細事宜。

♤ We'll deliver the goods within ten days.
我們將在十天內交貨。

♤ We can't accept orders during the product show.
在展示期間，我們不接受任何訂單。

♤ Sorry, ***these products are not for sale.***
很抱歉，這些都是非賣品。

♤ ***I assure you that it's a good bargain.*** 我保證您的訂購絕對合算。

**

latest〔ˈletɪst〕*adj*. 最新的 ***branch office*** 分公司
advise〔ədˈvaɪz〕*v*. 通知 bargain〔ˈbɑrgɪn〕*n*. 成交；廉售

♤ We've taken orders of one million dollars ***during the display fair***. 在展出期間，我們已經接了一百萬美元的訂單。

要求顧客

♤ ***Could you wait a moment***? I'll get an interpreter.
請您稍等一下好嗎？我去找位翻譯員。

♤ I'm sorry. These jewels are only for showing, you can't take them out.
對不起，這些珠寶只供觀賞，不可以拿出來。

♤ Pardon? 對不起，我沒聽清楚。

♤ Would you please repeat it again? 請您再說一次好嗎？

♤ ***Excuse me***, but please don't sit on the display shelf.
對不起，請勿坐在展示架上。

**

fair〔 fɛr 〕*n*. 商展　interpreter〔 ɪn'tɝprɪtɚ 〕*n*. 翻譯員
jewel〔'dʒuəl 〕*n*. 珠寶　repeat〔 rɪ'pit 〕*v*. 再說一次；重覆

附錄

參展必備語彙

- exhibition cost 參展費用　move-in hours 進場時間
- move-out hours 撤離會場時間　show hours 展示時間
- ***venue***〔'vɛnju〕*n.* 集合地點　opening times 開放時間
- ***dates for set-up and dismantling*** 佈置及拆除日期
- standard size 標準尺寸　exhibit height 展示高度（之限制）
- cashier's desk 出納櫃台　***information desk*** 資詢櫃台

- food service 餐飲服務　***lost and found*** 失物招領
- first-aid station 急救服務站　public telephone 公用電話
- ***security***〔sɪ'kjʊrətɪ〕*n.* 警備處
- registration〔,rɛdʒɪ'streʃən〕*n.* 登記處
- travel arrangements 旅遊服務　film theater 視聽室
- show office 會場辦公室　***age limitation*** 年齡限制

- advisory board 顧問群　membership meeting 會員大會
- press room 印刷服務室　***video equipment*** 視聽設備
- show sample label 展示樣品標簽
- buyers' guide 客戶指南　***show management*** 主辦單位
- daily schedule of events 每日活動表

CHAPTER

5

為個人和公司設計形象

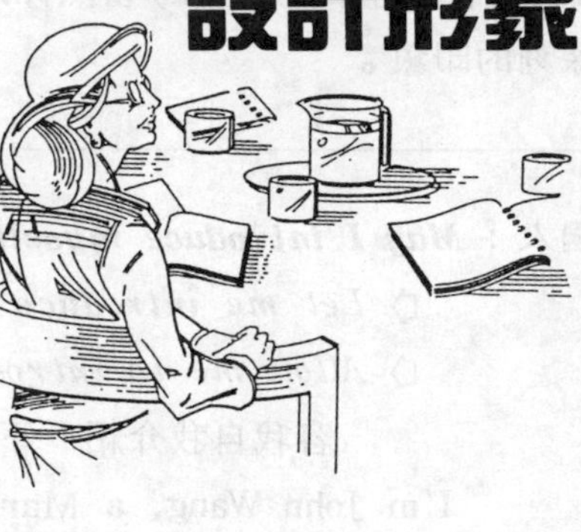

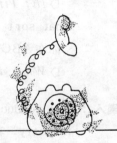

1. May I introduce myself?

我可以自我介紹嗎？

● **One Point Advice**

May I introduce myself？是**自我介紹**最好的開場白；不但可以馬上抓住對方的注意力，又可適時地道出自己的身分。對方爲了回禮，一定也會報上自己的大名。這時你不妨交換彼此的名片：***Here's my card.***（這是我的名片。）當然你的談吐必須**從容有禮**，才能讓對方留下深刻的印象。

中國人：***May I introduce myself***？我能自我介紹一下嗎？

⇨ *Let me introduce myself.* 讓我自我介紹一下。

⇨ *Allow me to introduce myself.*
容我自我介紹一下。

I'm John Wang, a Marketing Manager at ABC Company.
我是王約翰，ABC公司的行銷經理。

外國人：***I'm glad to meet you***, Mr. Wang.
很高興見到你，王先生。

I'm Tim Jackson. 我是提姆・傑克森。

⇨ *Hi, Tim Jackson.* 嗨，提姆・傑克森

What sort of work do you do at ABC?
你在ABC公司從事什麼樣的工作呢？

⇨ *What do you do there*？你在那裡從事什麼工作？

中國人：I'm conducting a market survey on the information industry. 我主持一個資訊工業的市場調查。

外國人：Oh, really? I'm with the New York liaison office.
哦，眞的？我在紐約的聯絡處工作。

中國人：***Here's my card***, and if I can do anything for you, ***please don't hesitate to let me know.***
這是我的名片，如果有什麼需要我幫忙的事，請別猶豫，儘快讓我知道。

● **Notes**

introduce〔ˌɪntrəˈdjus〕*v.* 介紹　allow〔əˈlaʊ〕*v.* 容許
Marketing Manager 行銷經理　conduct〔kənˈdʌkt〕*v.* 主持；管理
survey〔sɝˈve〕*n.* 調查　industry〔ˈɪndəstrɪ〕*n.* 工業
liaison〔ˌlieˈzɔ̃〕*n.* 聯絡　hesitate〔ˈhɛzəˌtet〕*v.* 猶豫

Hint Bank — 介紹公司實用語彙

- *think tank* 智囊團　*reception desk* 接待處
- subsidiary〔səbˈsɪdɪˌɛrɪ〕*n.* 附屬公司
- *name card* 名片
- *guest book* 訪客名册
- surname〔ˈsɝˌnem〕*n.* 姓（＝*family name*）

2. How are you?

你好嗎？

● **One Point Advice**

與人見面的第一句話，通常就是以***How are you***？（你好嗎？）來相互**問安**。在這種情況下，你也必須回答***I'm fine, thank you, and you***？（我很好，謝謝，那你呢？）。這雖是一種客套禮貌的問候，但切記不要流於俗套，落入**會話公式**中。因此最好不要**重覆**別人的問話，多加些變化，顯示較有誠意。

外國人：Good morning, Mr. Wang. How are you?
早安，王先生。你好嗎？

中國人：Fine, thanks. And you? 很好，謝謝。你呢？

外國人：***Nice to meet you again.*** 很高興再見到你。
⇨ *Good to see you again.* 很高興再見到你。
⇨ *Happy to see you again.* 很高興再見到你。

中國人：I haven't seen you for a long time.
我已經很久沒見過你了。

外國人：***How's everything with you?*** 工作情況如何？
⇨ *How're things going?* 最近好嗎？
⇨ *How's it going?* 近來可好？
⇨ *How're you doing?* 最近如何？

中國人： Everything's fine, thank you. 一切都好，謝謝你。

➪ *Fine, couldn't be better*. 很好，再好不過了。

And you？你呢？

外國人： ***Everything's the same***. 還是老樣子。

● **Notes**

for a long time 很久　***couldn't be better*** 再好不過

Hint Bank－公司內部組織

- *public relations department* 公關部
- *office of the President* 總經理室
- *general affairs department* 總務部
- *personnel department* 人事部
- *planning department* 企劃部
- *export department* 出口部
- *import department* 進口部

3. How do you do.

你好嗎？

● **One Point Advice**

初次與人見面時，要熟記 ***Shake-hand game*** 的應對用語。由於這必須是出於自然的舉動，所以**反應**必須很快，嘴中說出 ***How do you do.***（你好。），就趕快將手伸出準備握手。這個動作和說話的時間只有20秒。平常要多練習，到時才不會慢半拍。

中國人：***How do you do***, Mr. Brown? I'm John Wang from ABC Company.

你好嗎，布朗先生？我是ABC公司的王約翰。

外國人：I'm glad to meet you, Mr. Wang. 很高興見到你，王先生。

⇨ *I'm very happy to meet you.* 很高興見到你。

➪ *Glad to meet you.* 很高興見到你。

➪ *Nice to meet you.* 很高興見到你。

➪ *Pleased to meet you.* 很高興見到你。

中國人：I've ***been looking forward to*** meeting you.

我一直希望見到你。

外國人：I've ***heard*** a lot about you ***from*** Mr. White. It's nice to ***make your acquaintance.***

我從白先生那兒，聽說許多有關你的事。很高興認識你。

● Notes

pleased〔plizd〕*adj.* 高興的　***look forward to*** 希望；期望
make someone's acquaintance 與某人熟識

Hint Bank — 公司內部職位名稱

- *corporate advisor* 顧問　*chief accountant* 會計主任
- *chairman of the board* 董事長
- *general manager* 總經理
- *assistant manager* 協理
- *sales manager* 業務經理
- *branch manager* 分公司經理
- *sales engineer* 銷售工程師
- *sales representative* 業務代表
- *chief engineer* 總工程師　*sub manager* 襄理

4. I would like to meet Mr. ～

我想見～先生

● One Point Advice

因爲業務上的關係，你想主動認識客戶的工作伙伴時，不妨就大方地請客戶爲你引見：***I would like to meet Mr. Taylor. or Will you introduce me to Mr. Taylor?*** 這樣不但可令你**廣結善緣**，又可表示出你對客戶的**尊重**。

中國人： Mr. Brown, ***I would like to meet*** Mr. Taylor, your assistant. 布朗先生，我想見你的助理，泰勒先生。

➪ *Will you introduce me to Mr. Taylor?*

你能爲我介紹泰勒先生嗎？

➪ *Would you mind introducing me to...*

你不介意爲我介紹…

➪ *Could you introduce me to...*

你能幫我介紹…

外國人： Certainly. In fact, I've been planning to.

當然。事實上，我一直這麼打算。

What time would be convenient for you to come?

你什麼時候方便過來？

➪ *When is it convenient...*

什麼時候方便…

中國人： How about at two this afternoon?

今天下午兩點鐘如何？

外國人：All right. Please come and visit our office at two.
　　好的。兩點鐘請到我辦公室來。

中國人：***Fine, with pleasure***. Then, I'll see you at two.
　　好的，我很樂意。那麼，兩點鐘見。

● Notes

assistant〔ə'sɪstənt〕*n.* 助理　　convenient〔kən'vinjənt〕*adj.* 方便的
pleasure〔'plɛʒɚ〕*n.* 樂意；愉快

Hint Bank－介紹公司實用語彙

- *date of birth* 出生日期　*middle age* 中年
- *VIP* 重要人物（＝*very important person*）
- *all walks of life* 各界人士　*boy wonder* 青年才俊
- *fair-weather friend* 酒肉朋友
- *gate-crasher* 不速之客

5. Let me introduce ～

讓我來介紹～

● One Point Advice

當別人爲你引見辦公室的同事時，**握手**與**微笑**是最好的國際禮儀。千萬不要擺出 ***dead fish*** 的樣子；尚未開口就令人生厭。熟記一些應對的句型，如 ***It's a pleasure to meet you.*** 或 ***Nice to meet you.*** 等並加以活用；最好不要老是用相同的句子來應對；而顯得毫無誠意。

外國人：Let me introduce you to the people in the office.
讓我介紹你認識辦公室裡的人。

⇨ *I'd like you to meet my friend.*
我希望你見見我的朋友。

中國人：Fine. 好的。

外國人：Mr. Wang, this is my assistant, Bob Taylor.
王先生，這是我的助理，鮑伯・泰勒。

中國人：***It's a pleasure to meet you***, Mr. Taylor.
很榮幸認識你，泰勒先生。

外國人：Now I'd like you to meet my secretary, Miss Linda Simpson. 現在讓你認識我的祕書，琳達・辛普森小姐。

祕　書：Pleased to meet you, Mr. Wang. 很高興認識你，王先生。

中國人：Nice to meet you. 很高興認識你。

⇨ *The pleasure is mine.* 這是我的榮幸。

外國人：Mr. Wang, I would like to introduce two very important people here at DEF Company.

王先生，我想介紹兩位DEF公司內非常重要的人。

This is Miss Lisa Hudson, who is ***in charge of*** marketing research, and this is Mr. Bob Jackson, the assistant manager of the Sales Division.

這是麗莎·哈德遜小姐，是負責市場研究；這是鮑伯·傑克森，營業部門的副經理。

● Notes

secretary〔ˈsɛkrə,tɛrɪ〕*n.* 祕書　***in charge of*** 負責
research〔rɪˈsɝtʃ〕*n.* 研究　manager〔ˈmænɪdʒɚ〕*n.* 經理
Sales Division 營業部門

Hint Bank－介紹實用語彙

- *business running* 經商　*shorthand typist* 速記員
- *10 Outstanding Young Men* 十大傑出青年
- *governmental employee* 公務員
- *white-collar worker* 白領階級
- *blue-collar worker* 藍領階級
- *occupational disease* 職業病
- *middle class* 中產階級
- *career woman* 職業婦女
- *office girl* 女職員

6. Glad to have met～

很高興認識～

● **One Point Advice**

簡單地說聲 ***Good-bye*** 並不是唯一的道別方式，如果你能加上一句：***Thank you for all your help***. 就更能表現出你的風度和**禮貌**。除此之外，在你回去之後，可以再以一封簡短的 ***Thank you letter*** ；上面寫著：***Thank you very much for everything you've done during my stay in the United States***. 來增進彼此的情誼，讓你與客戶成爲眞正的朋友。

中國人：Goodbye, Mr. Brown. 再見，布朗先生。
I'm very glad to have met you. 非常高興認識你。
⇨ *It was very nice meeting you*. 很高興與你見面。
⇨ *Nice to have met you*. 很高興認識你。

外國人：Goodbye, Mr. Wang. 再見，王先生。
See you next week. 下星期見。
⇨ *See you Friday*. 星期五見。
Looking forward to our next meeting. 期待下次會面。

中國人： Sure, see you then. 當然，到時候見。

Thank you for all your help. 謝謝你的幫忙。

⇨ *Thanks for everything you did for me.*

謝謝謝你爲我做的一切。

外國人： ***Thank you for your time.*** 謝謝你抽空來。

● Notes

look forward to 期待　***see you then*** 到時候見

Hint Bank －介紹公司實用語彙

- *honor guest* 貴賓　*attend guest* 陪客
- *office hours* 營業時間　*branch office* 分公司
- *sales network* 銷售網　*head office* 總公司
- *corporate image* 企業形象　*semiannual bonus* 年中紅利
- *family enterprise* 家族企業　*parent company* 母公司
- *subsidiary company* 子公司
- *five-day workweek* 上班五天制
- *business community* 商界
- *corporate culture* 公司風氣
- *employment compensation* 失業保險
- *belt-tightening management* 減產經營

7. Have you heard of our company?

你聽過我們公司？

● **One Point Advice**

適時地爲別人介紹自己的公司，是塑立良好企業形象的第一步。首先你必須熟悉公司內部的**經營史**，並且將最値得驕傲的**事蹟**介紹給對方。一個能讓員工自豪並全心投入的公司，相信一定會獲得客戶的信賴。上班族不妨就以這句：***Have you heard of our company***？開始爲你的公司**促銷**吧。

中國人：***Have you heard of our company before***？

你以前聽過我們的公司嗎？

➪ *Do you happen to know our company*?

你知道我們的公司嗎？

➪ *Perhaps you're acquainted with our firm.*

或許你知道我們的公司。

外國人：I heard about your company often.

我常聽說有關貴公司的事。

➪ *I've read about your firm in newspapers.*

我曾在報紙上，讀過有關貴公司的報導。

➪ *I got the name of your company from a friend.*

我從朋友那兒聽說過貴公司。

Your company is well-known ***all over the world.***

貴公司世界聞名。

When was your company founded? 貴公司何時創立的？

中國人： Our company was established in 1899 as the first Chinese joint-venture company with a Western partner.

我們的公司創設於一八九九年，是中華民國第一家與西方夥伴合資的公司。

⇨ *Our company was founded about ninety years ago.*
我們的公司大約在九十年前創立。

⇨ *Our company will soon celebrate its ninetieth anniversary.* 我們的公司不久就要慶祝九十週年了。

● Notes

be acquainted with 知道；熟識　　firm〔fɝm〕*n*. 公司
well-known〔'wɛl'non〕*adj*. 有名的　　found〔faʊnd〕*v*. 創立
establish〔ə'stæblɪʃ〕*v*. 創設　　***joint-venture company*** 合資公司
anniversary〔,ænə'vɝsərɪ〕*n*. 週年紀念

Hint Bank — 介紹公司實用語彙

- *main plant* 主要工廠　　*office equipment* 辦公設備
- *electrical appliance* 電化製品
- *industrial area* 工業區　　*labor union* 工會

8. Who is the founder of ABC?

ABC的創始人是誰？

● **One Point Advice**

有些客戶會主動詢問公司的經營狀況，作爲判斷公司的標準，這時你若一問三不知；那麼臉就丟大了。若是在歷史較悠久的國際公司；你不妨對它的**創辦人**、各個部門的**營業項目**、**交易產品**等多加了解。只要平時多用心注意，一旦客戶再問起：***Do you know who the founder of ABC is***？你就可侃侃而談了。

外國人：***Do you know who the founder of ABC is***？

你知道ABC公司的創辦人是誰嗎？

中國人：Yes, Mr. Edward Chao. 是愛德華・趙先生。

外國人：From what company did ABC receive technological assistance in its early days？

早期的ABC公司，是從哪個公司接受科技支援呢？

中國人：It was linked with North Electronic Company in the United States.

它是與美國的北方電子公司結合的。

外國人：What was initially produced at that time？

當時一開始是製造什麼東西呢？

⇨ *What were the main products*...？主要產品是什麼…？

⇨ *What sort of products did you import*...？

你們進口哪一類的產品？

⇨ *What sort of products did you deal with?*
你們買賣哪一類產品呢？

中國人：ABC assembled telephone sets ***in its infancy.***
ABC公司初期組合電話零件。

外國人：In what field is ABC regarded as a leading manufacturer?
在哪一領域內，ABC公司被認爲是主要製造商？

中國人：In the field of telecommunications.
在電信通訊方面。

外國人：I see. 我明白了。

● Notes

founder〔'faʊndɚ〕*n.* 創辦人　　initially〔ɪ'nɪʃəlɪ〕*adv.* 最初地
technological〔,tɛknə'lɑdʒɪkl̩〕*adj.* 科技的
assemble〔ə'sɛmbl̩〕*v.* 組合　　infancy〔'ɪnfənsɪ〕*n.* 初期；幼年

Hint Bank－企業經營實用語彙

- conglomerater〔kən'glɑmərɪtɚ〕*n.* 複合企業團
- *channels of distribution* 經銷管道
- *electronic equipment* 電子儀器
- turnover〔'tɝn,ovɚ〕*n.* 營業量
- *data processing* 資料處理

9. One of the leading manufacturers

主要製造商之一

● One Point Advice

美國的財星（***Fortune***）雜誌，每年都會爲世界各大企業票選排行榜。可見名列前茅的優良製造商一定是最好的宣傳利器，大企業自然可以：***Our company is one of the leading manufacturers in the R.O.C.***（我們公司是中華民國主要的製造商之一。）而中小企業也不妨以：***Our company has grown remarkably in the past three years.***（本公司在過去三年中成長快速。）來提高公司形象。

中國人：As you know, our company is one of the leading manufacturers in the R.O.C.

如您所知的，我們公司是中華民國主要的製造商之一。

⇨ *Our company is the largest printer* ...

我們公司是最大的印刷廠…

⇨ *Our company is the third largest auto company*...

我們公司是第三大的汽車公司…

外國人：***How many employees do you have***？你們有多少員工？

中國人：We have about 60,000 employees including those working in our affiliates.

我們大約有六萬名員工，包括分公司的員工在內。

More than 3,000 travel all over the world, with about 1,000 residing abroad.

超過三千人在世界各地推銷，其中有一千人住在國外。

外國人：Well, ***I'm surprised*** to hear how huge an enterprise ABC is.

嗯，聽到ABC公司是如此大的企業，我很驚訝。

Where is your head office？你們的總公司在哪兒？

中國人：In Taipei. 在台北。

● **Notes**

manufacturer〔,mænjə'fæktʃərɚ〕*n.* 製造商　printer〔'prɪntɚ〕*n.* 印刷廠
auto company 汽車公司　employee〔ɪm'plɔɪ·i, ,ɛmplɔɪ'i〕*n.* 員工
affiliate〔ə'fɪlɪ,et〕*n.* 分公司　reside〔rɪ'zaɪd〕*v.* 居住
travel〔'trævl̩〕*v.* 出外推銷；旅行　enterprise〔'ɛntɚ,praɪz〕*n.* 企業

Hint Bank－產業介紹實用語彙

- *office automation equipment* 辦公室自動化設備
- *multinational enterprise* 多國企業
- *growth industry* 成長工業
- budget〔'bʌdʒɪt〕*n.* 預算
- *developing countries* 開發中國家
- *recreation facilities* 娛樂設施

10. Where is your biggest market?

你們最大的市場在哪裡？

● **One Point Advice**

市場佔有率一直是公司業績的指標。因此某些初次接洽的代理商一定會關心產品在市場上的銷售情形。台灣的貿易多以外銷爲主，印著"***made in Taiwan***"的產品更是隨處可見。這時你就可說：***We export all over the world.***（我們外銷到全世界。）或***We do business in thirty countries.***（我們和三十個國家有生意往來。）

外國人：Where is the biggest market for your broadcasting equipment? 你們的廣播器材，最大的市場在哪兒？

中國人：Our ***primary market*** is the R.O.C.
我們的主要市場在中華民國。

外國人：Which countries does your company export to?
你們公司外銷到哪些國家？

中國人：***We export all over the world***, but we do a lot of our business in Asia.
我們外銷到全世界，但我們在亞洲的生意很大。
Our trade with Southeast Asia is growing.
我們在東南亞的市場正在擴大。

➪ *Our main area of activity is in the States.*
我們主要的活動區域在美國。

➪ *We do business in thirty countries.*
我們和三十個國家有生意往來。

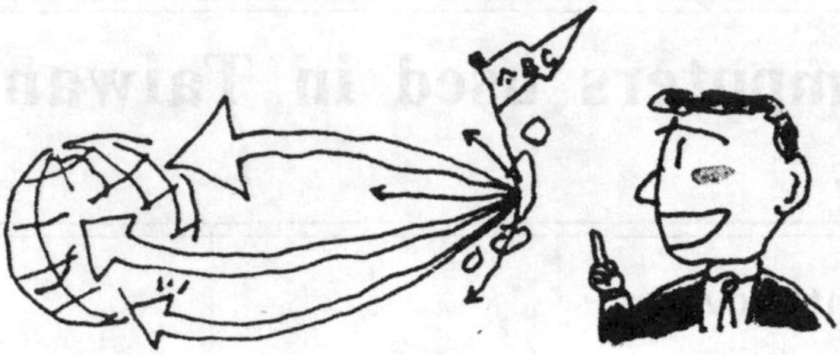

▷ *We cover the States west of the...*

我們涵括了美西的…

外國人： I see. You export your products to Asia, too.

我明白了。你們也對亞洲出口產品。

中國人： Yes, that's right. We have been supplying many color and black and white transmitters to Asian countries.

沒錯。我們提供許多彩色及黑白的發報機給亞洲國家。

● Notes

broadcasting equipment 廣播器材

primary〔'praɪ,mɛrɪ, -mərɪ〕*adj*. 主要的

export〔ɪks'port, 'ɛksport〕*v*. 外銷

supply〔sə'plaɪ〕*v*. 提供；供應

transmitter〔træns'mɪtɚ〕*n*. 發報機

Hint Bank－市場介紹實用語彙

- *labor movement* 勞工運動　*labor market* 勞動市場
- competition〔,kɑmpə'tɪʃən〕*n*. 競爭
- competitor〔kəm'pɛtətɚ〕*n*. 競爭者
- labor-saving〔'lebɚ,sevɪŋ〕*adj*. 省力的
- *technological revolution* 科技革命

11. Computers used in Taiwan

電腦在台灣

- **One Point Advice**

電腦業在台灣是個新興的尖端科技工業，從電腦公司增加的速度來看，電腦業正是處於蓬勃發展的時期。在台灣，電腦的使用已相當普遍，從辦公室的大型全套**自動化系統**到小型**個人電腦**，其市場皆相當看好。一般的電腦公司多以能獨立**開發**軟體產品爲傲，這時，你可說 ***In recent years we have developed a variety of computer systems.***（最近幾年，我們已開發了許多電腦系統。）

外國人： What about the development of your computer department? 你們的電腦部門發展如何？

中國人： In 1953, our company ***started to study computer systems in Taiwan.***

在一九五三年，我們公司開始在台灣研究電腦系統。

In recent years we have developed a variety of ABC computer systems.

最近幾年，我們已開發了許多ABC電腦系統。

外國人： It must have been an important business decision for a Taiwanese enterprise to ***go into the computer manufacturing field*** at that time.

在那個時候，對一個台灣的企業，要進入電腦生產的領域必然是個重要的貿易決定。

中國人： Yes. It was really a difficult situation, I suppose.
是的。我想，那的確是個艱難的處境。

外國人： ABC produced the first transistorized general purpose computer system, didn't it?
ABC公司製造了第一個電晶體化的多功能電腦系統，不是嗎？

中國人： That's right. Since then ABC ***has ranked as*** one of the leading computer manufacturers in Taiwan.
是的。從那以後ABC公司就列入中華民國主要電腦製造商之一。

● Notes

development〔dɪ′vɛləpmənt〕*n*. 發展　***computer department*** 電腦部
a variety of 許多　decision〔dɪ′sɪʒən〕*n*. 決定
situation〔,sɪtʃʊ′eʃən〕*n*. 處境　suppose〔sə′poz〕*v*. 想像
transistorized〔træn′zɪstə,raɪzd〕*adj*. 電晶體化的
general purpose 多功能的　rank〔ræŋk〕*v*. 列入

Hint Bank－電腦實用語彙

- bit〔bɪt〕*n*. 數元　*BPI* 字元吋（＝*Byte per Inch*）
- block〔blɑk〕*n*. 版段
- *data channel* 資料通道
- *cylinder index* 磁柱指標
- hardware〔′hɑrd,wɛr〕*n*. 硬體
- software〔′sɔft,wɛr〕*n*. 軟體

12. What's your market share?

你們的市場分配如何？

● **One Point Advice**

在注重包裝的工商企業中，**推銷**掛帥早已不足爲奇。利用媒體來塑造公司或產品的形象更是今後台灣轉型經濟的重點。一般而言**電視**廣告（***TV commercials***）、**雜誌**及**報紙**的廣告（***advertisements in newspapers and magazines***）最能達到效果。上班族若能加以應用，必能提高銷售業績，創造更高的利潤。

外國人：What's your market share for your broadcasting equipment? 你們的廣播器材市場分配如何？

⇨ *What's the total amount of your annual sales?*
你們的年銷總量爲多少？

中國人：ABC has supplied broadcasting equipment to more than 60% of the broadcasting stations in the R.O.C.
ABC公司提供廣播器材給中華民國超過百分之六十的廣播電台。

外國人：***What kind of*** advertising have you been using for your products? 你們的產品使用什麼方式的廣告？

中國人：We're constantly running ads in newspapers, popular magazines and trade journals
我們不斷在報紙，暢銷雜誌，及商業刊物上登廣告。
We advertise on TV, too. 我們也用電視廣告。

外國人：***TV commercials are one of the most effective means of advertising.*** 電視廣告是最有效的廣告方式之一。

中國人：That's right. ***We set aside a large portion of our budget for advertising.***

是的。我們保留預算的一大部分，作爲廣告之用。

● Notes

share〔ʃɛr〕*n.* 分配　total〔'totl̩〕*adj.* 總計的
annual〔'ænjuəl〕*adj.* 年度的；每年的　***broadcasting station*** 廣播電台
advertising〔'ædvɚ,taɪzɪŋ〕*n.* 廣告　constantly〔'kɑnstəntlɪ〕*adv.* 不斷地
trade journal 商業刊物　effective〔ə'fɛktɪv, ɪ-〕*adj.* 有效的

Hint Bank — 公司行政實用語彙

- *fiscal year* 會計年度　*sister company* 姊妹公司
- *advertising expense* 廣告費用
- *board of directors* 董事會
- *trade liberalization* 自由化貿易
- *company limited by shares* 股份有限公司

附錄

台灣各大企業英文名稱

- 南亞塑膠工業 / NAN YA PLASTICS CORP.
- 台灣塑膠工業 / FORMOSA PLASTICS CORP.
- 台灣化學纖維 / FORMOSA CHEMICALS & FIBER CORP.
- 大同 / TATUNG CO. LTD.
- 遠東紡織 / FAR EASTERN TEXTILE, LTD.
- 裕隆汽車製造 / YUE LOONG MOTOR CO., LTD.
- 統一企業 / PRESIDENT ENTERPRISE CORP.
- 三陽工業 / SAN YANG INDUSTRY CO., LTD.
- 台灣松下電器 / MATSUSHITA ELECTRIC (TAIWAN) CO., LTD.
- 中興紡織廠 / CHUNG SHING TEXTILE CO., LTD.
- 福特六和汽車 / FORD LIO HO MOTOR COMPANY LTD.
- 台灣飛利浦電子工業 / PHILIPS ELECTRONICS INDUSTRIES (TAIWAN) LTD.
- 台灣水泥 / TAIWAN CEMENT CORPORATION
- 聲寶 / SAMPO CORPORATION
- 永豐餘造紙 / YUEN FOUNG YU PAPER MFG. CO., LTD.
- 東元電機 / TECO ELECTRIC & MACHINERY CO., LTD.
- 味全食品工業 / WEI CHUAN FOODS CORP.
- 亞洲水泥 / ASIA CEMENT CORP.
- 光陽工業 / KWANG YANG INDUSTRY CO., LTD.
- 台元紡織 / TAI YUEN TEXTILE CO., LTD.
- 台灣王安電腦 / WANG LABORATORIES (TAIWAN) LTD.
- 台灣聚合化學品 / USI EAST CORPORATION

- 中華汽車工業／
  CHINA MOTOR CO., LTD.
- 艾德蒙海外／
  AOC INTERNATIONAL
- 台灣慧智／
  WYSE TECHNOLOGY TAIWAN, LTD.
- 中國力霸／
  CHINA REBAR CO., LTD.
- 台灣通用器材／
  GENERAL INSTRUMENTS OF TAIWAN LTD.
- 太子汽車工業／
  PRINCE MOTORS CO., LTD.
- 味王／
  VE WONG CORPORATION
- 台灣凱普電子／
  CAPETRONIC(TAIWAN) CORP.
- 三商行／
  MERCURIES AND ASSOCIATES LTD.
- 明台產物保險／
  MINGTAI FIRE & MARINE INSURANCE CO., LTD.
- 南山人壽保險／
  NAN SHAN LIFE INSURANCE CO., LTD.
- 瑞士商吉時洋行／
  GETZ BROS. & CO., INC. (TAIPEI BRANCH)
- 台灣日立／
  TAIWAN HITACHI CO., LTD.
- 中華賓士汽車／
  CAPITAL MOTORS INC.
- 三井工程／
  SAH CHING ENGINEERING CO., LTD.
- 新光產物保險／
  SHIN KONG FIRE & MARINE INSURANCE CO., LTD.
- 太平產物保險／
  THE TAI PING INSURANCE CO., LTD.
- 華僑產物保險／
  MALAYAN OVERSEAS INSURANCE CORPORATION
- 太平洋建設／
  PACIFIC CONSTRUCTION CORP., LTD.
- 台灣日立電視工業／
  HITACHI TELEVISION (TAIWAN) LTD.
- 台灣玻璃工業／
  TAIWAN GLASS IND. CORPORATION
- 福壽實業／
  FU SOW GRAIN PRODUCTS CO., LTD.
- 台灣有力電子／
  UNIDEN CORPORATION OF TAIWAN
- 迪吉多電腦／
  DIGITAL EQUIPMENT TAIWAN, LTD.
- 台灣花王／
  TAIWAN KAO CO., LTD.

- 歌林／
  TAIWAN KOLIN CO., LTD.
- 新力／
  SHINLEE CORPORATION
- 新光紡織／
  SINKONG SPINNING CO., LTD.
- 黑松／
  HEI SONG CORPORATION
- 宏碁電腦／
  ACER INDUSTRIAL CORP.
- 中興電工機械／
  CHUNG-HSIN ELECTRIC MACHINERY MFG. CO., LTD.
- 李長榮化學工業／
  LEE CHANG YUNG CHEMICAL INDUSTRY CORP.
- 嘉新水泥／
  CHIA HSIN CEMENT CORP.
- 功學社／
  KUNG HSUE SHE CO., LTD.
- 泰山企業／
  TAI SHAN ENTERPRISE CO., LTD.
- 三芳化學工業／
  SAN FANG CHEMICAL INDUSTRY CO., LTD.
- 台灣增你智／
  ZENITH TAIWAN CORPORATION
- 亞洲聚合／
  ASIA POLYMER CORPORATION
- 潤泰工業／
  RUENTEX INDUSTRIES LTD.
- 濟業電子／
  GREAT ELECTRONICS CORP.
- 台達化學工業／
  TAITA CHEMICAL CO., LTD.
- 聯華電子／
  UNITED MICROELECTRONICS CORP.
- 士林紙業／
  SHIHLIN PAPER CORP.
- 中國唯一製衣廠／
  CHINA UNIQUE GARMENTS MFG. CO., LTD.
- 大台北區瓦斯／
  THE GREAT TAIPEI GAS CORP.
- 南僑化學工業／
  NANCHOW CHEMICAL INDUSTRIAL CO., LTD.
- 台灣東菱電子工業／
  TOBISHI ELECTRONIC INDUSTRIES (TAIWAN) LTD.
- 國聯工業／
  FORMOSA UNITED INDUSTRIAL CORP., LTD.
- 達新工業／
  TA HSIN INDUSTRIAL CORP.
- 台榮產業／
  TAI RONG PRODUCTS CO., LTD.
- 光男企業／
  KUNNAN ENTERPRISE LTD.

- 台灣史谷脫紙業／
TAIWAN SCOTT PAPER CORP.
- 永大機電工業／
YUNGTAY ENGINEERING CO., LTD.
- 中國人造纖維／
CHINA-MADE FIBER CORPORATION
- 台旭纖維工業／
TAI SHIH TEXTILE INDUSTRY CORP.
- 養樂多／
YAKULT CO., LTD.
- 台灣理光／
TAIWAN RICOH CO., LTD.
- 華通電腦／
COMPAQ MANUFACTURING CO., LTD.
- 台灣普利司通／
BRIDGESTONE TAIWAN CO., LTD.
- 台灣勝家實業／
SINGER INDUSTRIES (TAIWAN) LTD.
- 台灣必治妥／
BRISTOL-MYERS (TAIWAN) LIMITED
- 嘉裕／
CARNIVAL TEXTILE INDUSTRIAL CORPORATION
- 台灣資生堂／
TAIWAN SHISEIDO CO., LTD.
- 滙豐汽車／
FORTUNE MOTORS CO., LTD.
- 南寶樹脂化學工廠／
NAN PAO RESINS CHEMICAL CO., LTD.
- 台灣船井電機／
FUNAI ELECTRIC CO. OF TAIWAN
- 和益化學工業／
FORMOSAN UNION CHEMICAL CORP.
- 詮腦電子／
COPAM ELECTRONICS CORPORATION
- 國泰人壽保險／
CATHAY LIFE INSURANCE CO., LTD.
- 新光人壽保險／
SHIN KONG LIFE INSURANCE CO., LTD.
- 長榮海運／
EVERGREEN MARINE CORP.
- 國產汽車／
CHINESE AUTOMOBILE CO., LTD.
- 南陽實業／
NAN YANG INDUSTRIES CO., LTD.
- 高林實業／COLLINS CO.,LTD.
- 遠東百貨／
FAR EASTERN DEPARTMENT STORES LTD.
- 國泰產物保險／
CATHAY INSURANCE COMPANY LTD.
- 神通電腦／MITAC INC.

● 心得筆記欄 ●

CHAPTER

6

電話熱線的魅力

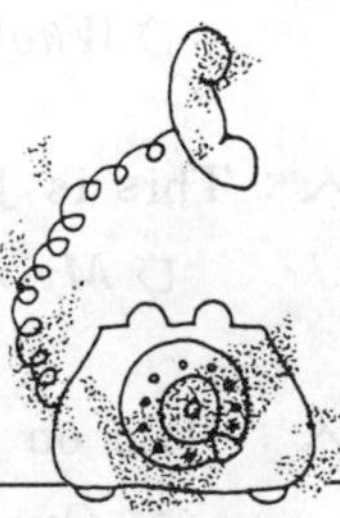

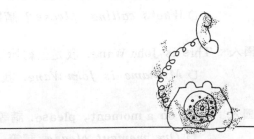

1. Is this the White residence?

這是白公館嗎？

● **One Point Advice**

當你打私人電話給外國客戶時，一抓起聽筒你知道該怎麼說嗎？首先你必須有禮貌地**確定**有沒有打錯電話：***Is this the White residence?***（這是白公館嗎？）如果要找的人不在家中，記得千萬不可馬上就掛上電話，一定要請對方**留言**或留下自己的名字：***Could I leave a message?***（我可以留個話嗎？）這樣才不會令人感到突兀失禮。

中國人：Hello. ***Is this the White residence?***
喂，這是白公館嗎？

外國人：Yes, it is. 是的。

中國人：Could I speak to Mr. Peter White, please?
請找白彼得先生聽電話，好嗎？
⇨ *Is Peter in?* 彼得在家嗎？

外國人：I'm not sure if he is in right now, but whom shall I say is calling, please?
我不確定他現在是否在家，請問您是哪位？
⇨ *Who's calling, please?* 請問您是哪位？

中國人：This is John Wang. 我是王約翰。
⇨ *My name is John Wang.* 我是王約翰。

外國人：Hold on a moment, please. 請等一下。
⇨ *One moment please.* 請等一下。

I'm sorry, he is not home. 很抱歉，他不在家。

⇨ *He is out, sorry.* 他出去了，抱歉。

中國人：***Could I leave a message?*** 我可以留個話嗎？

外國人：Certainly. Let me write it down.

當然。讓我記下來。

中國人：Ask him to call me as soon as he gets back.

請他回去後儘快打電話給我。

● Notes

residence〔ˈrɛzədəns〕*n.* 住宅

message〔ˈmɛsɪdʒ〕*n.* 留言；消息　***as soon as*** 儘快

Hint Bank－打電話實用語彙

- *public telephone* 公用電話　*telephone book* 電話簿
- *telephone booth* 電話亭　*area code* 區域號碼
- *telephone number* 電話號碼　*emergency call* 緊急電話
- *credit card call* 信用卡電話　*domestic call* 國內電話
- *telephone office* 電信局　*exchange number* 交換台號碼
- *conference call* 會議電話　*crossed lines* 電話干擾

2. We have a collect call from ~

有一通～打來的付費電話

● **One Point Advice**

接到一通國際電話（ ***international long-distance call*** ）時，一定要問明接線生是哪種電話。當你聽到：***We have a collect call from*** ～時，千萬不可隨口回答 ***Yes***，因爲這是一通請**受話人付費**的電話（ ***collect call*** ）。當然如果你願意接通的話，請說：***We'll pay for the call.***（我們會付費的。）

外國人： This is the United States calling. Is this 123-4321?
這裏是美國。請問是123-4321號嗎？

中國人： Yes, it is. ***May I help you***?
是的。需要我幫忙嗎？

外國人： ***We have a collect call for*** Mr. Wang from Mr. Williams in New York.
有一通紐約的威廉斯先生，打給王先生的付費電話。

中國人： A collect call for Mr. Wang from Mr. Williams in New York? May I have his Department?
紐約的威廉斯先生，打給王先生的付費電話嗎？請問他在什麼部門？

外國人： The Foreign Department. 國外部。

中國人： The Foreign Department? Just a moment, please.
國外部嗎？請等一下。

We'll pay for the call. 我們會付費。

⇨ *We'll accept the charges.* 我們會付費的。

Will you let me know the time and charges after the call？電話打完後，能否告訴我時間和費用呢？

外國人： Yes, we will. 會的。

中國人： Mr. Wang is on the line. ***Go ahead, please.***

王先生已接通了。請開始。

⇨ *Your section is on the line.*

你的部門已經接通了。

● **Notes**

collect call 付費電話　***Foreign Department*** 國外部

accept〔ək'sɛpt, æk-〕*v.* 接受　charge〔tʃɑrdʒ〕*n.* 費用

Hint Bank－電話實用語彙

- *person-to-person call* 叫人電話
- *station-to-station call* 叫號電話
- *overseas call* 國際電話　*direct-dial call* 直撥電話
- *long distance call* 長途電話　*local call* 市內電話

3. I'd like to talk to ~

我要和～說話

● One Point Advice

打電話到公司找人時，一定要把所要找的人的**名字**和**職位**說清楚。如果聽不清楚對方的英語，則必須有禮貌地請對方說慢一點：***Would you speak more slowly, please?*** 其實公司裏的商用電話都有一定的**格式**，只要熟練句型、加以活用，就可得心應手。

中國人： I'd like to talk to Mr. Brown in the Import Section.
我想和進口部門的布朗先生談話。
➪ *May I speak to*... 我能和…談話嗎？

接線生： Just a minute, please. 請稍候。
➪ *Hold up, please*. 請稍候。
Mr. Brown is on the line. 布朗先生已接通了。
➪ *You are connected now*. 已經接通了。

中國人： Thank you. Hello, Mr. Brown?
謝謝你。喂，布朗先生嗎？

回　答： I'm sorry, I think ***you've got the wrong number***. There's no one here by that name.
抱歉，我想你打錯了。這裏沒有這個人。

中國人： Then, will you give me extension 205?
那麼，能否幫我轉到二〇五分機？
➪ *May I have extension 205?* 可否接 205 分機？

接線生： Would you speak more slowly, please? 請說慢些，好嗎？

⇨ *Will you repeat that again*? 請再說一遍好嗎？

中國人： Extension 205, please. 請接二〇五分機。

接線生： 205? 二〇五？

中國人： ***That's right***. 是的。

接線生： The number is on the line. Go ahead, please.

號碼已經撥通了。請開始。

⇨ *The number doesn't answer*. 電話沒有人接。

● Notes

Import Section 進口部門　***on the line*** 接通

connect〔kəˈnɛkt〕*v.* 接通　***wrong number*** 打錯電話

extension〔ɪkˈstɛnʃən〕*n.* 分機

Hint Bank－電話實用語彙

- switchboard〔ˈswɪtʃˌbord〕*n.* 電話總機
- *mouth piece* 傳話機　*intercom system* 對講機系統
- *service meter* 通話次數表　*party line* 同線電話
- *wireless tranceiver* 無線電對講機
- *radio telephone* 無線電話　*coin call* 投幣電話

4. Making an appointment

安排約會

● **One Point Advice**

忙碌的上班族生活，講求的就是**效率**與**業績**。因此，用電話來安排約會時，記得不要扯得太遠。寒暄過後，就可進入正題，表明來意。在確定時間的時候，要注意必須**明確**地說出見面的時刻，如 ***at one***, ***at twelve***。而不要說出像 ***in the morning*** 這類的含糊時間。另外外國人喜歡利用午餐的時間，一邊用餐，一邊輕鬆地談生意。這種午餐叫做 ***business lunch***（商業午餐）。上班族不妨試試看。

外國人： Hello, Mr. Wang. How are you? What can I do for you?
喂，王先生。你好嗎？有什麼需要我效勞的？

中國人： I'm fine, thanks. I'd like to ***make an appointment*** to discuss our computer.
我很好，謝謝。我想約個時間，討論我們的電腦。

外國人： Very good. Do you want to come by today?
很好。你想今天來嗎？

中國人： Yes, if that's possible.
好啊，如果可能的話。

外國人： Let me see... yes, ***I'm free*** all afternoon.
我看看…好的，我整個下午都有空。

中國人： That sounds good. Shall I come at one?
那很好。我一點鐘來行嗎？

外國人： Why don't you come at noon and we'll have lunch together?

何不中午來，我們一起吃飯？

中國人： Fine, I'd like that. I'll see you at twelve then.

好，我喜歡那樣。那麼十二點鐘見。

外國人： Good. See you then. 好的。到時候見。

● Notes

appointment〔ə'pɔɪntmənt〕*n.* 約會　　discuss〔dɪ'skʌs〕*n.* 討論

Hint Bank－辦公室用具實用語彙

- memorandum〔,mɛmə'rændəm〕*n.* 備忘錄
- stapler〔'steplɚ〕*n.* 釘書機
- stamp〔stæmp〕*n.* 橡皮印章　　*gem clip* 迴紋針
- *paper punch* 打孔器　　*ash tray* 烟灰缸
- *carbon paper* 複寫紙　　*thumb tack* 圖釘
- *chit book* 便條本

5. Would you please spell the name?

請拼出名字好嗎？

● One Point Advice

在大一點的國際公司中，一般都會有總機**接線生**（*operator*）幫你轉接各個部門的電話。因此當你聽到接線生說：***Would you please spell the name***？時，最好能將受話人的名字拼出來，如果人名過長，則可要求接線生再**覆述**一遍，以免發生「搭錯線」的尷尬情形。

接線生：DEF Company. ***May I help you***?
DEF公司。需要我幫忙嗎？

中國人：Yes, please. May I talk to Mr. Brown?
是的。請幫我接伯朗先生聽電話？
▷ *Put me through to Mr. Brown.*
請接伯朗先生。

接線生：I beg your pardon? 請再說一遍好嗎？
▷ *Pardon*? 抱歉，再說一次好嗎？

中國人：Mr. Brown, please. 請接伯朗先生。

接線生：Would you spell the name, please?
請你拼出名字好嗎？
▷ *May I have the spelling, please*?
請用拼的，好嗎？

中國人：That's B—R—O—W—N.
是B—R—O—W—N。

接線生： B—R—O—W—N, correct? B—R—O—W—N, 是嗎？

中國人： That's right. 是的。

接線生： You are calling Mr. Brown in the Foreign Department?

你是找國外部的伯朗先生嗎？

中國人： Yes. 是的。

接線生： ***Thank you for waiting.*** 謝謝你耐心等候。

⇨ *I'm sorry to have kept you waiting.*

抱歉讓你久候。

He is on the line. Go ahead, please.

已接通了。請開始。

● Notes

spell〔spɛl〕*v.* 拼(某字)字母　　correct〔kə'rɛkt〕*adj.* 正確的

Hint Bank — 辦公室文具實用語彙

- *order book* 定貨簿　　*desk calendar* 座枱日曆
- *invoice book* 發貨簿　　*filing cabinet* 檔案櫃
- *scribbling pad* 草稿本
- stationery〔'stɛʃən,ɛrɪ〕*n.* 文具

6. Phoning for a flight reservation

電話預定機票

● One Point Advice

無論是出差或旅遊，「飛機」一向是上班族最滿意的選擇。因此用電話預訂機票則爲上班族完美出擊的第一步。***I'd like to make reservations for a flight to～***（我想訂到～的機位）爲最常用的句型。另外在出發前須記得再向航空公司 ***check*** 一次，或者請訂位員在班機更換時，隨時以電話通知你。以免造成遺「機」之憾。

訂位員： UA Reservations. May I help you?
聯合航空訂位組。需要我幫忙嗎？

中國人： ***I'd like to make reservations for a flight to Chicago.***
我想訂到芝加哥的機位。

訂位員： When will you be departing? 您幾時離開？

中國人： Around seven tonight. ***Are there any flights available around that time?***
大約今晚七點。那時候有沒有任何班次？

訂位員： How many tickets do you want? 您要幾張票？

中國人： Two seats, please. 請給我兩個位子。

訂位員： Two seats, Chicago, around seven... We have a flight leaving at 7:15 tonight.
兩個位子，芝加哥，七點左右…今晚七點十五分有一班次離開。

中國人： That will be fine. My name is John Wang, that's W—A—N—G, and I'll be with Mr. Tom Chang, C—H—A—N—G. 那很好。我的名字是王約翰，是W—A—N—G，和我同行的是張湯姆，是 C—H—A—N—G。

訂位員： Fine. Check-in will be thirty minutes before departure. 好。起飛前三十分鐘辦理登機手續。

中國人： Thank you. 謝謝你。

● Notes

reservation 〔ˌrɛzəˈveʃən〕*n*. 預訂　　depart 〔dɪˈpɑrt〕*v*. 離開
available 〔əˈveləbḷ〕*adj*. 可利用的　　seat 〔sit〕*n*. 座位

Hint Bank — 各大航空公司名稱

- *American Airlines* 美國航空　　*Lufthansa* 德國航空
- *China Airlines* 中華航空　　*Northwest Orient* 西北航空
- *Singapore Airlines Limited* 新加坡航空
- *Cathay Pacific Airway* 國泰航空
- *Garuda Indonesian Airways* 印尼航空
- *Japan Asia Airlines* 日亞航空
- *United Airlines* 聯合航空
- *Royal Dutch Airlines* 荷蘭航空

● 心得筆記欄 ●

CHAPTER

7

出差充電專輯

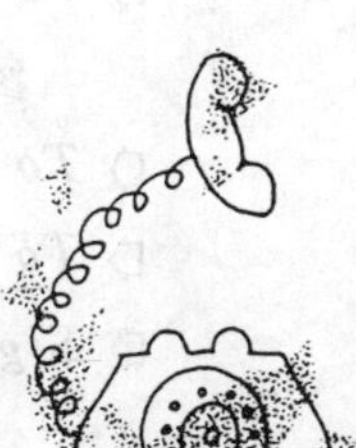

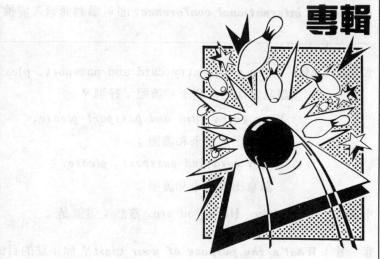

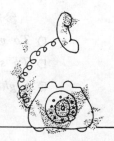

1. At the Immigration office

在入境室

● One Point Advice

當你抵達目的地的機場時，首先便是辦理**入境手續**（***Immigration***）。除了檢查**護照、簽證**是否有效，另外機場的官員通常會訊問你入境的「**目的**」和停留的「**期限**」。你只需簡要地回答清楚，如***Business.*** 或 ***To attend an international conference.*** 即可順利通過入境檢查。

官　員：May I see your entry card and passport, please?

請讓我看你的入境卡和護照，好嗎？

⇨ *Your entry card and passport please.*

請拿出入境卡和護照。

⇨ *Entry card and passport, please.*

請拿出入境卡和護照。

中國人：Certainly. Here you are. 當然。這就是。

官　員：***What's the purpose of your visit*** ? 你來訪的目的爲何？

中國人：Business. 洽商。

⇨ *To attend an international conference.*

參加一個國際會議。

⇨ *To visit some friends.* 拜訪幾個朋友。

⇨ *To study.* 讀書。

⇨ *Sightseeing.* 觀光。

官　員：I see. ***How long are you going to stay?***

我明白了。你準備待多久呢？

⇨ *How long will you be in the States?*

你會在美國待多久？

⇨ *How long do you intend to stay?* 你打算停留多久？

中國人：For about two weeks. 大約兩星期。

⇨ *Until the 15th.* 到十五號。

官　員：Good. That'll be all, thank you. 好。就這樣，謝謝你。

● Notes

passport〔'pæs,port, -,pɔrt〕***n.*** 護照　purpose〔'pɝpəs〕***n.*** 目的

attend〔ə'tɛnd〕***v.*** 參加　conference〔'kɑnfərəns〕***n.*** 會議

intend〔ɪn'tɛnd〕***v.*** 打算

Hint Bank — 機場實用語彙

- *waiting room* 候機室　*quarantine counter* 檢疫處
- *departure lobby* 走廊
- nationality〔,næʃə'nælətɪ〕***n.*** 國籍
- *registered domicile* 籍貫　*air ticket* 飛機票
- *certificates of vaccination* 黃皮書
- *baggage tag* 行李籤條　*ticket counter* 售票處
- *terminal building* 機場大廈
- *customs officer* 海關人員
- *passenger inspection* 旅客檢查

2. Your customs declaration, please.

請申報關稅。

● **One Point Advice**

各國海關爲防止毒品、武器的走私入境，在通關時皆會要求乘客將所攜帶的物品**申報**（*declare*）。如果所攜帶的物品需要報稅時，在飛機上便要先填好**申報卡**（*declaration card*）。如果是較貴重的禮物時，只需填上 ***personal effects*** 即可。一般而言，海關官員所問的都是一些固定的問題，事先若能準備好，即可安全通關。

官　員：Your customs declaration card, please.
請拿出你的關稅申報卡。

中國人：Here it is. 在這兒。

官　員：Do you have anything to declare?
你有任何要申報的東西嗎？

➪ *Don't you have anything to declare?*
你沒有要申報的東西嗎？

中國人：I don't think so, ***I have only personal effects.***
我想沒有，我只有一些私人物品。

➪ *These are my personal belongings.*
這些是我的私人物品。

官　員：Please open your bags. 請打開你的袋子。

中國人：All right. There you are. 好的。這就是。

官　員：You have two cameras. Are they German cameras?
你有兩部照相機。是德國相機嗎？

中國人：Yes, they are. 是的。

官　員：Since they are both of the same make, ***only one camera is exempted from tax.*** You'll have to pay the customs duty on the second one. Please take your card and pay the cashier.
由於它們是同一廠牌的，只有一部相機可以免稅。你必須付第二部相機的關稅。請拿你的申報卡向出納員付款。

● Notes

declaration〔,dɛklə'reʃən〕*n.* 申報（書）　camera〔'kæmərə〕*n.* 照相機
make〔mek〕*n.* 廠牌；製造方法　exempt〔ɪg'zɛmpt, ɛg-〕*v.* 使免除
tax〔tæks〕*n.* 稅　***customs duty*** 關稅
cashier〔kæ'ʃɪr〕*n.* 出納員

Hint Bank－兌換錢幣迷你情報

＊離開機場前，別忘了作三件事：

①校對當地時間。
②兌換當地錢幣。
③與有關航空公司機場櫃台確定（*confirm*）下一站機票。

・Yen〔jɛn〕*n.* 日幣　*HK$* 港幣（＝*Hong Kong dollar*）
・Sterling〔'stɝlɪŋ〕*n.* 英幣　*U.S. dollar* 美金
・*JMP* 人民幣（＝*Jen Min Pi*）　Franc〔fræŋk〕*n.* 法郎
・*NT$* 新臺幣　Greenback〔'grin,bæk〕*n.* 美鈔
・*Deutsche Mark* 德國馬克　Rouble〔'rubḷ〕*n.* 盧布

3. Getting a taxi

搭計乘車

● **One Point Advice**

出國在外，如欲搭計程車時，最好先問清楚當地是否有 ***taxi stand***（**計程車招呼站**）。因爲在某些地方，是不准隨意招呼計乘車的。在上車前，應該把目的地告訴司機，如果怕對方聽不清楚，可將目的地寫在紙條上，如"***Holiday Inn***"，"***Santa Clara***"，再遞給司機。

中國人：***Where can I catch a taxi***？哪裡可以叫到計程車？

⇨ *Where can I find the taxi stand*？
哪裡有計程車招呼站？

⇨ *Where is the taxi stand*？計程車招呼站在哪裡？

服務台：The taxi zone is right on the left corner over there.
計程車招呼站就在左邊轉角處。

中國人：Are you free？您有空嗎？

司　機：Sure. Where are you going？當然。您要去哪裡？

中國人：To Santa Clara. 到聖塔・克萊拉。

司　機：Santa Clara？ O.K. That's about 30 miles away.
聖塔・克萊拉？好的，大約是三十哩遠。

中國人：***How much will it cost***？需要多少錢呢？

司　機：That'll run about $50.00. 大約五十美元。

中國人：That's O.K. 沒問題。

● **Notes**

catch a taxi 叫計程車　　run〔rʌn〕*v.* 花費

Hint Bank－交通工具迷你情報

在市區，除了搭計程車之外，捷運地下鐵（*Mass Transit Subway*）和巴士（*bus*）也是很便利的交通工具。在日本、法國等地，地下鐵可通往市區的各個角落。而在美國，greyhound bus（灰狗巴士）更是隨處可見，是美國人主要交通工具之一。出差時，若需短程往返，可利用之。另外，若是欲從機場到市區的旅館，可利用機場內，開往鄰近市區的 Limousine bus（交通車）。

4. Do you have a reservation?

您有預定嗎？

● **One Point Advice**

無論是業務出差或私人旅遊，住宿的安排往往是煞費周章。尤其在觀光旺季時，更必須及早預訂房間。通常旅行社都會有訂房的服務，若是出差時，能請**分公司**及**客戶**代爲訂房，那就方便多了。到了飯店之後，只要向櫃台人員報上你的大名及訂房的方式，即可 ***check in***。

辦事員：Good afternoon, sir. ***Do you have a reservation***?
午安，先生。您有預定嗎？

中國人：Yes, I made a reservation through ABC America.
是的，我是經由美國的ABC公司預定的。

辦事員：May I have your name, sir? 能告訴我你的名字嗎，先生？

中國人：My name is John Wang. 我是王約翰。

辦事員：I'll check the reservation book. Yes, here it is. Mr. Wang of ABC. A single room with bath is reserved for you. Will you register here, please?
我查一下預定的册子。有了，在這兒。ABC公司的王先生。已經幫你留了一間有浴室的單人房。請在這裡登記好嗎？
⇨ *Would you fill this out*? 請塡寫這份表格好嗎？

中國人：All right. 好的。

辦事員：You'll be staying for a week?

你將停留一個星期嗎？

中國人：Yes, that's right. I'll be leaving on Monday morning.

是的，沒錯。我將在星期一早上離開。

辦事員：Your room is 665 on the 6th floor. ***The bellboy will show you the way.***

你的房間是六樓的六六五號房。服務生會帶你去。

中國人：Thank you. 謝謝你。

● **Notes**

reservation〔,rɛzə'veʃən〕*n.* 預定；預約　register〔'rɛdʒɪstə〕*v.* 登記
fill out 塡寫　bellboy〔'bɛl,bɔɪ〕*n.* 服務生；侍者

Hint Bank－住宿實用語彙

· motel〔mo'tɛl〕*n.* 汽車旅館　inn〔ɪn〕*n.* 小旅館
· *reservation counter* 預約櫃台
· deposit〔dɪ'pɑzɪt〕*n.* 訂金
· hotel〔ho'tɛl〕*n.* 旅館
· *room service* 客房服務部
· *one night stay* 住宿一晚
· *room number* 房間號碼　*arrival date* 抵達日期
· *departure date* 出發日期　*pay first* 先付款

5. Laundry service

洗衣服務

● One Point Advice

如果需要旅館提供**洗、燙衣服**的服務時，需向 ***laundry service*** 問清楚送洗和取回的時間、地點。若是衣物因質料不同而需要特別處理或洗濯時，則事先應告知服務人員。如 ***I'd like this garment dry-cleaned, please.***（這件衣服要乾洗），或 ***I'd like to have my suit pressed.***（請幫我燙這件西裝。）

服務員：May I help you？需要我幫忙嗎？

中國人：***I want to have some shirts washed.*** Will you pick them up, please？

我有些襯衫需要洗。能否請你來拿取？

服務員：Yes, sir. May I have your name and room number, please？好的，先生。請告訴我您的姓名和房間號碼，好嗎？

中國人：Wang. Room 665. 姓王，六六五號房。

服務員：If you're in a hurry, ***we can have them ready for you tonight***. 如果您急著要的話，我們今天晚上就可以弄好。

中國人：If I can have them by tomorrow morning, that will be fine. 只要在明天早上弄好就可以了。

服務員：Very well, sir. Is there anything else? 很好，先生。還有別的事嗎？

中國人：No, that's all. Thank you. 沒有，就這樣了。謝謝你。

• Notes

laundry〔'lɔndrɪ, 'lɑn-〕*n.* 衣服之洗燙

pick something up 拿取某物　　***in a hurry*** 匆忙地

Hint Bank－洗燙服務實用語彙

- jeans〔dʒinz〕*n. pl.* 牛仔衣褲　　*dry cleaning* 乾洗
- roommaid〔'rum,med〕*n.* 整理房間的女僕
- bleaching〔'blitʃɪŋ〕*n.* 漂白
- valet〔'vælɪt〕*n.* 男僕
- *clear starch* 上漿
- sweater〔'swɛtɚ〕*n.* 毛衣
- underwear〔'ʌndɚ,wɛr〕*n.* 內衣褲
- *no ironing* 免燙　　*coin-up laundry* 投幣洗衣機

6. I'm checking out.

我要結帳。

● One Point Advice

辦理**結帳退宿**叫做 ***check out*** 。住宿費用的計算是從早上到翌日中午十二點爲一天，所以應在一大早就將行李整理好。一般旅館都有替客人提行李的**服務生**（ ***bellboy*** ），因此在離開旅館時，也可以電話召喚服務生爲你搬提行李。如 ***Could you send a bellboy to Room～?*** （能不能派一位服務生到～號房來？），不過別忘了給 ***bellboy* 小費**（ ***tip*** ）以表示謝意。

中國人： ***Could you send a bellboy to room*** 665？

能不能派一位服務生到六六五號房來？

辦事員： Certainly, sir. He'll be up in a couple of minutes.

當然，先生。他幾分鐘內就會上去。

服務生：（ Knocks at the door ）（敲門）

中國人： Yes. Come in. Please take these suitcases. I'll take my briefcase. 請進。請替我拿這些皮箱。我自己拿公事包。

▷ *I'd like to have my bags taken down to the lobby right away*. 我想把袋子立刻拿到大廳去。

服務生： Very good, sir. 好的，先生。

辦事員： Good morning, sir. 早安，先生。

中國人： Good morning. ***I'd like to check out now.***

早安。我想現在結帳。

辦事員：May I have your key, please? You stayed three nights and made 12 local and 3 long distance telephone calls.
請給我您的鑰匙，好嗎？您住了三晚，並打了十二通市內電話及三通長途電話。

中國人：***That sounds about right***. 應該沒錯。

辦事員：All right, sir. That comes to $300 including tax.
好的，先生。含稅總共三百美元。

● **Notes**

check out 結帳退宿　　***a couple of minutes*** 幾分鐘
suitcase〔'sut,kes,'sjut-〕*n*. 皮箱；小提箱
briefcase〔'brif,kes〕*n*. 公事包　　lobby〔'lɑbɪ〕*n*. 大廳
local call 市內電話　　***long distance call*** 長途電話

Hint Bank — 旅館付帳實用語彙

- *EMERGENCY EXIT* 緊急出口　　*by card* 簽信用卡
- *extra key* 備用鑰匙　　*by cash* 付現金
- *hotel charges* 旅館費用　　*by check* 付支票

7. Could you tell me how to get to～

你能告訴我如何到～？

● One Point Advice

在國外**問路**是出差的上班族共有的經驗，許多人往往不是不知如何開口，便是被老外的**左彎右拐**弄得暈頭轉向。如果是你身處在陌生的異國街道時，你知道該怎麼辦嗎？最保險的方法是——準備一張**地圖**，隨時向路人問明你所在的地點，如***Would you show me on this map where I am right now***？如此一來，你就可按圖索驥，暢通無阻了。

中國人：Could you tell me how to get to the head office of ABC？請問到ABC公司的總公司該怎麼走？

➪ *How do I get to the head office*？

我該怎麼到總公司？

➪ *How can I get to the...*？

我該怎麼到…？

➪ *Where're ABC's headquarters from here*？

ABC公司的總部在哪兒？

外國人：Let's see. Do you know the XYZ River？

我看看。你知道XYZ河嗎？

中國人：No, I arrived from Taiwan only a week ago.

不，我一星期前才從台灣來的。

Would you show me on this map where I am right now？

你能否告訴我，在這張地圖上，我所在的位置？

外國人： Sure. Let's see...yes, you are right here.

當然。我看看…對了，你就在這裡。

You go straight down this street.

你順著這條街一直走下去。

➪ *Walk straight down this street.*

順著這街一直走下去。

➪ *Go straight down here.* 從這兒一直走下去。

中國人： Thank you very much. 非常謝謝你。

● Notes

head office 總公司　headquarters〔'hɛd'kwɔrtəz, -,kw-〕*n. pl.* 總部

go straight 一直走

Hint Bank — 道路交通實用語彙

- *pedestrians crossing* 行人穿越道　*left turn* 左轉
- sidewalk〔'saɪd,wɔk〕*n.* 人行道　*no passing* 禁止穿越
- *road signs* 交通標誌　*make a detour* 繞行
- *take a short cut* 抄近路

8. Having dinner alone in a restaurant

獨自在餐廳用餐

● **One Point Advice**

國外的餐館一般皆有**侍者**（*waiter*）負責帶位，若是暫時沒有空位時，侍者會告訴你：***All of our tables are taken right now.*** 並且詢問你是否願意稍等一會兒。點菜時，如果你點的是牛排，就要告訴 ***waiter*** 你要幾分熟。全熟是 ***well-done***、五分熟是 ***medium***、未完全煮熟則為 ***rare***。若是你喜歡三、四分熟，則說 ***medium rare***。

侍　者：Good evening. How many in your party?
　　晚安。請問有幾位？

中國人：Just myself. 就我一人。

侍　者：***All of our tables are taken right now.***
　　我們所有的桌位都滿了。
　　But if you'd care to wait, we can seat you soon.
　　但如果您願意等的話，我們很快就能幫您找個座位。

中國人：All right. I'll wait. 好的。我願意等。

侍　者：Fine. I'll call you as soon as a table is available.
　　好。一有桌位我馬上叫你。
　　……

侍　者：***Your table is ready now.*** 您的桌位已弄好了。
　　Here's the menu. 這是菜單。

中國人：I'd like the sirloin steak dinner, please.
請給我牛腰肉牛排。

侍　者：Fine. Which vegetable, please? 好的。請問要什麼菜？

中國人：A baked potato and green beans. 烤馬鈴薯和豌豆。

侍　者：***How would you like your steak cooked***?
您要幾分熟的牛排？

中國人：***Medium rare***. 五分熟。

侍　者：All right, sir. Thank you. 好的，先生。謝謝您。

● Notes

restaurant〔'rɛstərənt, -,rɑnt〕*n*. 餐館　　menu〔'mɛnju〕*n*. 菜單
sirloin〔'sɝlɔɪn〕*n*. 牛腰上部之肉

Hint Bank－用餐實用語彙

- tableware〔'tebḷ,wɛr〕*n*. 餐具　　*dining table* 餐桌
- knife〔naɪf〕*n*. 刀子　　tablecloth〔'tebḷ,klɔθ〕*n*. 桌巾
- saucer〔'sɔsɚ〕*n*. 茶碟；小碟　　fork〔fɔrk〕*n*. 叉子
- spoon〔spun〕*n*. 湯匙　　plate〔plet〕*n*. 盤子

9. I'd like to eat meat dishes.

我想吃些肉食料理。

● **One Point Advice**

在餐館中應邀作客時，若不知道該點些什麼，可向侍者或主人徵求建議，如***What would you recommend***？或***Any Suggestions***？另外在與人共餐時，須先問清楚對方是否對某些食物有特別的喜好或厭惡。在國外，有些人流行吃**素食**(***vegetarian meal***)，這時你可適時地對他說：***No wonder you are healthy***！（難怪你這麼健康！）

主　人：What would you like？您想吃什麼？

⇨ *What would you like to order*？您想點什麼？

⇨ *What do you feel like having*？您想吃什麼？

⇨ *What'll you have*？您想吃什麼？

客　人：***What would you recommend***？你推薦什麼？

⇨ *What do you suggest*？你建議什麼？

⇨ *Any suggestions*？有什麼建議嗎？

主　人：Do you like meat？您喜歡肉食嗎？

　　　　◇ *Do you care for meat*？您喜歡肉食嗎？

客　人：Yes, I do. I'd like to try one of their meat dishes.

　　　　是的，喜歡。我想試試他們的肉食料理。

主　人：Then, why don't you have the filet？

　　　　那麼，何不試試肉片？

　　　　◇ *How about the filet*？肉片怎麼樣？

客　人：***That sounds good.*** 聽起來不錯。

● Notes

recommend〔ˌrɛkəˈmɛnd〕*v.* 推薦　　suggest〔səˈdʒɛst〕*v.* 建議

filet〔fɪˈle, ˈfɪle〕*n.* 肉片；魚片

Hint Bank－用餐實用語彙

- ***quick lunch*** 快餐　　mutton〔ˈmʌtn̩〕*n.* 羊肉
- chicken〔ˈtʃɪkən〕*n.* 雞肉　　turkey〔ˈtɝkɪ〕*n.* 火雞
- ***table d'hote*** 客飯
- pork〔pork〕*n.* 豬肉
- ***sea food*** 海產食物
- pudding〔ˈpʊdɪŋ〕*n.* 布丁
- bouillon〔ˈbʊljɑn, bujˈɔ〕*n.* 牛肉湯
- specialty〔ˈspɛʃəltɪ〕*n.* 招牌菜

10. My stomach became upset.

我的胃有點不舒服。

● **One Point Advice**

上班族在外國出差時，難免會因爲飲食起居的改變而引起**腸胃方面**的疾病。這時候，你知道該如何向醫生描述病情嗎？其實只要一句：***My stomach became upset all of a sudden.***（我的胃突然痛了起來。）即可清楚地表達。在美國，醫生只負責開**處方**（***prescription***），病人必須拿著處方到藥局去付錢買藥。不過出門在外，能儘量注意身體的健康而不生病當然最好。

醫　生：What's seems to be the problem? 有什麼問題嗎？

　⇨ *What's the trouble?* 怎麼了？

病　人：***My stomach became upset all of a sudden.***

　我的胃忽然痛了起來。

醫　生：All right. Please take off your shirt.

　好的。請脫下襯衫。

　Have you had any trouble with your stomach before?

　你的胃以前有過毛病嗎？

病　人：No. Never. 不，從沒有。

醫　生：***You have a slight case of indigestion.*** I think you're probably working too hard.

　你有輕微的消化不良。我想你可能工作過度了。

It's not serious and it should clear up shortly.

不太嚴重，很快就會好了。

病　人：That's good. 那很好。

醫　生：I'll make out a prescription for you.

我會爲你開一份處方。

And you should watch what you eat for a few days.

這幾天你得留意你的食物。

Eat mild foods and stay away from greasy, fried foods.

吃清淡的食物，避免油膩，油炸的食品。

Take care. 當心些。

病　人：Thank you, I will. 謝謝你，我會的。

● Notes

take off 脫下　　***all of a sudden*** 突然地

indigestion〔,ɪndə'dʒɛstʃən, ,ɪndaɪ-〕*n*. 消化不良

prescription〔prɪ'skrɪpʃən〕*n*. 處方；藥方　　greasy〔'grisɪ, 'grizɪ〕*adj*. 油膩的

Hint Bank －就醫實用語彙

- headache〔'hɛd,ek〕*n*. 頭痛　　*no appetite* 食慾不佳
- *catch a cold* 感冒　　allergy〔'ælɚdʒɪ〕*n*. 過敏症
- *feel feverish* 發燒
- *eye drop* 眼藥水
- toothache〔'tuθ,ek〕*n*. 牙痛
- *sleeping pill* 安眠藥
- *sore throat* 喉嚨痛　　cough〔kɔf〕*v*. 咳嗽

11. Renting a car

租車

● **One Point Advice**

在海外出差，尤其是美國，能租到一輛車來代步，那是最好不過了。但是在租車時，一定要攜帶 ***International Driver's Licence***（**國際駕照**）及 ***ID***（***Indentification*** ——**身分證明**）。另外爲了安全起見，最好能先**保險**（***insurance***），通常保險費都已包括在租車的費用中。

顧　客：***I'd like to rent a car tomorrow***, for a day, please.
我明天想租一天車子。

店　員：O.K. Which would you like, a compact or a sedan?
好的。你喜歡什麼樣子，小汽車還是轎車。

顧　客：***How much is a compact car for a day***?
小汽車租一天多少錢？

店　員：It's fifteen dollars a day and fifteen cents a mile, sir. 一天十五元，一哩十五分，先生。

顧　客：Does that include insurance? 包括保險嗎？

店　員：Yes, sir. It includes insurance and a full tank of gas, too. 是的，先生。包括保險也包括滿滿一箱汽油。
May I see your driver's license?
我可以看看你的駕照嗎？

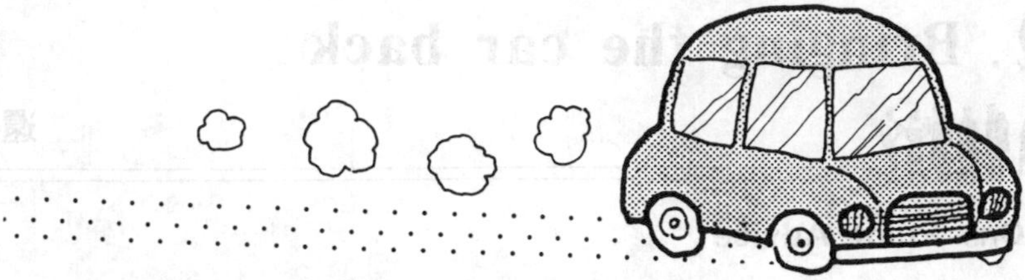

顧　客：***Here it is***. I have an International Driver's License. 在這裡。我有國際駕照。

店　員：Here's your license, and would you fill out this form please? 這是你的駕照，請你填一下這張表格好嗎？

顧　客：Certainly. 當然。

● **Notes**

compact〔ˈkɑmpækt〕*n*. 小型汽車　　sedan〔sɪˈdæn〕*n*. 轎車

include〔ɪnˈklud〕*v*. 包括　　tank〔tæŋk〕*n*. 油箱

Hint Bank－租車實用語彙

- automobile〔ˈɔtəmə,bil, ,ɔtəˈmobɪl, ,ɔtəməˈbil〕*n*. 汽車
- *sports car* 跑車　　*convertible car* 敞篷汽車
- *station wagon* 旅行客貨車　　rally〔ˈrælɪ〕*n*. 越野車
- *air-conditioned car* 冷氣車　　truck〔trʌk〕*n*. 卡車
- *mileage per mile* 每哩費用　　jeep〔dʒip〕*n*. 吉普車
- *vehicle accident insurance* 交通意外保險

12. Bringing the car back

還車

● **One Point Advice**

談妥租車的費用時，接著便是提車的問題。如果當場不付款提車，租車店員便會向你要求先付一部分**保證金**（*deposit*），這時別忘了要張**收據**（*receipt*），做爲提車的憑證。至於歸還時，因爲一般的租車公司都在當地遍設辦事處，所以不必把車開回原公司，只要歸還任何一家辦事處卽可，非常方便。

顧　客：***I want to pick up the car*** tomorrow morning at seven. Are you open then?
　　我想在明天早上七點提車。那時你們開門了嗎？

店　員：Yes, we are, Mr. Wang. Would you like to pay now?
　　是的，王先生。你要現在付款嗎？

顧　客：I think I'll pay when I return the car because I may use it for more than a day. Is that all right?
　　我想還車時再付，因爲我可能不只用一天。可以嗎？

店　員：That's all right but ***we require a deposit***.
　　可以，但我們要求保證金。

顧　客：***How much is it***？多少呢？

店　員：Fifty dollars in advance. 先付五十元。

顧　客：O.K., but could you give me a receipt?

好的，但能否給我一張收據呢？

店　員：Certainly. Here it is. 當然。這就是。

顧　客：Thank you. 謝謝你。

● **Notes**

pick up 提取　　return〔rɪ'tɝn〕*v.* 歸還

require〔rɪ'kwaɪr〕*v.* 要求　　deposit〔dɪ'pɑzɪt〕*n.* 保證金

in advance 預先地　　receipt〔rɪ'sit〕*n.* 收據

Hint Bank — 行車駕駛實用語彙

- *turn off engine* 熄火　　*press horn* 按喇叭
- *step on accelerator* 踩油門　　*parking fee* 停車費
- *parking meter* 停車收費器　　*rush hours* 尖峰時間
- *multi-storied garage* 立體停車場
- *emergency brake* 緊急剎車　　*traffic volume* 交通量
- *happy driving* 一路平安

13. At the bank

在銀行

● **One Point Advice**

在海外生活，身懷大筆現金總是危險且不便。這時你可向當地的銀行開戶。一般分為 ***savings account***（**儲蓄存款戶頭**）和 ***checking account***（**活期存款戶頭**）兩種。其中 ***checking account*** 較合乎需要，因為你可以用**支票**付款，而不必攜帶大筆現金。每個月末，銀行即會送來你的收支明細表，非常方便。

中國人：***I'd like to open a bank account***. 我想開個銀行戶頭。

職　員：A savings account or a checking account?
儲蓄存款戶頭還是活期存款戶頭？

中國人：Could you explain the difference between the two?
你能否解釋兩者有何不同？

職　員：Certainly. A savings account bears 4% interest per year. 當然。儲蓄存款戶頭每年負擔百分之四的利息。
A checking account does not bear any interest but you can pay your bills ***by check***. You don't have to carry large amounts of cash.
活期存款戶頭不負擔任何利息，但你可以支票付款。你不須攜帶大筆現金。

中國人：I see. I'd like to open a checking account then.
我明白了。那麼我要開活期存款戶頭。

職　員：***By all means***. That's what most Americans do.
當然。多數美國人都這麼做。

中國人：***Is there a charge for it***？需付費用嗎？

職　員：If your checking account balance is more than $200, there is no charge.
如果你的活期存款戶頭餘額超過二百元，就不需費用。

中國人：I'd like to deposit $2,500 in a checking account.
我想存進二千五百元到活期存款戶頭裡。

職　員：Would you fill out these forms？
請你填這些表格好嗎？

● Notes

account〔ə'kaʊnt〕*n.* 戶頭；帳戶　　interest〔'ɪntrɪst〕*n.* 利息
bill〔bɪl〕*n.* 帳單　　charge〔tʃardʒ〕*n.* 費用
deposit〔dɪ'pazɪt〕*v.* 存放；儲存

Hint Bank 一銀行實用語彙

- *dishonored check* 空頭支票　　*signature card* 印鑑卡
- *trust fund* 信託資金
- *district bank* 地方銀行
- *deposit certificate* 存款單
- *account closed* 帳戶結清

14. At the post office

在郵局

● One Point Advice

出差時，總免不了到郵局去**郵寄包裹**或**信件**，因此上班族也應該熟記一些基本用語，如***I'd like to mail this package.***（我要郵寄包裹。）另外，由於各國郵局的作業程序不同，所以一遇到不清楚的時候，最好加上一句：***What's it for***？（這是做什麼用的？）請郵局職員爲你解釋清楚。

中國人：Excuse me. ***I'd like to mail this package to Taiwan,*** and buy some stamps.
抱歉。我想寄這包裹到台灣，並買些郵票。

職　員：You can do both right here. 兩樣都可以在這兒辦理。
Would you fill out this green customs sticker?
請先填這張綠色關稅貼紙好嗎？

中國人：What should I write here? 我該在這兒寫些什麼呢？

職　員：What's in the package? 包裹裡是什麼？

中國人：Three books. 三本書。

職　員：O.K. Write " three books " here and write down the value, too. 好的。在這兒寫下「三本書」，並寫下其價格。
You also have to fill out this white sticker.
你還要填這張白色貼紙。

中國人：***What's it for***？這是做什麼用的？

職　員：This is to indicate what you want done with the package if it doesn't reach the addressee.

這是指示如果物件未達收件人，你要如何處理這包裹。

中國人：I'd like it returned to me. 我希望歸還給我。

職　員：***In that case***, check the box "return to sender".

那樣的話，在「歸還寄件人」那一格上做記號。

● Notes

package〔ˈpækɪdʒ〕*n*. 包裹　stamp〔stæmp〕*n*. 郵票
sticker〔ˈstɪkɚ〕*n*. 貼紙　indicate〔ˈɪndəˌket〕*v*. 指示；指出
addressee〔ˌædrɛsˈi〕*n*. 收件人

Hint Bank — 郵局實用語彙

- *surface mail* 普通郵件　*air mail* 航空郵件
- *sea mail* 海運郵件　*special delivery mail* 限時專送
- *registered mail* 掛號　envelope〔ˈɛnvəˌlop〕*n*. 信封
- *return postcard* 回郵明信片　*ordinary mail* 平信
- *postal remittance* 郵政劃撥　*zip code* 郵遞區號

15. Need some help?

需要幫忙嗎？

● One Point Advice

大一點的國際公司通常擁有很多不同的部門，因此你在作業務拜訪時，就會有摸不著門路的煩惱。這時你不妨留意身旁經過的職員，請他幫忙帶路，但是可別忘了向他**道謝**：***Thanks. You've been a big help.*** 雖然這只是隨口的一句話，卻能夠爲你建立良好的第一印象，做個受歡迎的上班族。

職　員：Do you need some help? 你需要幫忙嗎？

　　⇨ *Can I help you*? 我能幫你嗎？

　　⇨ *May I help you*? 我能幫你嗎？

中國人：Yes, ***I'm looking for*** the Trading Division.

　　是的，我在找貿易部門。

　　⇨ *Can you tell me how to get to the...*

　　　你能告訴我如何到…嗎？

　　⇨ *I'm trying to find...* 我在找…

　　⇨ *Whereabouts is the ...* 附近哪裏有…

職　員：Just walk straight and turn left over there.

　　直直走，在那兒左轉。

　　⇨ *You have to turn left over there.*

　　　你必須在那兒左轉。

　　⇨ *Just take a right over there.* 就在那兒右轉。

中國人：Thanks. ***You've been a big help.***

謝謝。你幫了我大忙。

➪ *Thank you for your help.* 謝謝你的幫忙。

➪ *Thanks. I appreciate the help.*

謝謝。很感激你的幫忙。

● Notes

look for 尋找　　whereabouts〔ˌhwɛrəˈbaʊts〕*adv.*〔疑問詞〕約在哪裏

appreciate〔əˈpriʃɪˌet〕*v.* 感激

Hint Bank－客套寒喧實用語彙

- I haven't seen you for a long time. 好久不見了。
- How are you? 你好嗎？
- How do you do. 你好。
- Everything's the same. 還是老樣子。
- How's everything with you? 近來如何？
- Fine, couldn't be better. 很好，再好不過了。

16. I'm sorry, I don't know.

對不起，我不知道。

● One Point Advice

當你在國外時，突然遇到外國人向你**問路**時，千萬要弄清楚 ***I don't know*** 和 ***I don't understand*** 的區別。如果你自己也是外地人而不知道他所問的問題，這時你要說：***I don't know. I'm a stranger myself.*** 而不是 ***I don't understand***，這句話是說我**聽不懂**（對方的語言），有要求再說清楚一點的意思。

中國人：***Excuse me***, but where's the Japan Culture Center?

抱歉，日本文化中心在哪兒呢？

➪ *Which way to the Japan Culture Center?*

哪一條路到日本文化中心？

外國人：I'm sorry. I don't know. I'm a stranger myself.

很抱歉。我不知道。我自己也是外地人。

➪ *Sorry, can't help you.*

抱歉，無法幫你。

Why don't you ask the man over there?

你何不問問那裡的那個人？

➪ *I suggest you ask someone else.*

我建議你問問別人。

➪ *You should ask that man over there.*

你應該問問那裡的那個人。

中國人：Thanks, ***just the same***. 還是要謝謝你。

（To another person：）（向另一個人：）

Pardon me. Is the Japan Culture Center in this area?

抱歉。日本文化中心是不是在這一區？

● Notes

culture〔'kʌltʃɚ〕*n.* 文化　　area〔'erɪə〕*n.* 地區

stranger〔'strendʒɚ〕*n.* 陌生人

Hint Bank－建築物實用語彙

- mansion〔'mænʃən〕*n.* 大厦　　***storied house*** 樓房
- bungalow〔'bʌŋgə,lo〕*n.* 平房　　***arcade room*** 騎樓房
- skyscraper〔'skaɪ,skrepɚ〕*n.* 摩天大樓
- apartment〔ə'pɑrtmənt〕*n.* 公寓
- residence〔'rɛzədəns〕*n.* 住宅　　***double deck*** 樓中樓
- building〔'bɪldɪŋ〕*n.* 大樓　　***official residence*** 官邸
- hallway〔'hɔl,we〕*n.* 走廊　　***tatami house*** 日本房屋

17. Exchange traveller's checks

兌換旅行支票

● One Point Advice

在海外兌換旅行支票（ ***Traveller's checks*** ）時，銀行會向你要求**身分證明**文件（ ***identification*** ），這時你必須出示**護照**或**國際駕照**。在兌換時要先問清楚目前的兌換比率是多少：***What's the exchange rate today***？如果你想兌換一些零錢，也必須事先說明。

中國人： ***I'd like to cash some traveller's checks here.***

我想在這兒兌換一些旅行支票。

⇨ *Can I cash a traveler's check?*

我能兌換旅行支票嗎？

⇨ *Do you cash traveler's checks?*

你這兒能兌換旅行支票嗎？

⇨ *I'd like to convert some NT dollars to U.S. dollars, please.* 請幫我將一些新台幣兌換為美金。

職　員： Certainly. Do you have any identification?

當然。你有任何證明文件嗎？

中國人： Yes, I have my passport. Here it is.

是的，我有護照。這就是。

職　員： Fine. How much would you like to exchange, sir?

好的。您要兌換多少呢，先生？

⇨ *How much do you want to exchange?*

您要兌換多少？

中國人：***What's the exchange rate today***？目前兌換比率多少？

職　員：A dollar is valued at twenty eight NT dollars.

一美金價值二十八元新台幣。

中國人：Fifty dollars, please. 請換五十元。

Could you give me one dollar in small change？

能否給我一元的小面額零錢？

職　員：Here you go, sir. Will that be all right？

在這兒，先生。那樣可以嗎？

● Notes

cash〔kæʃ〕*v.* 兌現；兌付　　***traveller's check*** 旅行支票

convert〔kən'vɜt〕*v.* 兌換　　identification〔aɪ,dɛntəfə'keʃən〕*n.* 身分證明

passport〔'pæs,port, -,pɔrt〕*n.* 護照　　exchange〔ɪks'tʃendʒ〕*v.* 兌換；交換

change〔tʃendʒ〕*n.* 零錢

Hint Bank－銀行業務實用語彙

- ***blank check*** 空白支票　　***dishonored account*** 拒絕往來戶
- passbook〔'pæs,bʊk〕*n.* 活期存摺　　***past due*** 過期
- deficit〔'dɛfəsɪt〕*n.* 赤字　　***enquiry desk*** 詢問處
- endorsement〔ɪn'dɔrsmənt〕*n.* 背書

18. At the shop

在商店中

● **One Point Advice**

出差的上班族總免不了會在當地購買一些**禮物**分送親友；這時最常說的一句話便是：**這個多少錢**？（***How much is it*？ *or What's the price*？**）國人一般都有討價還價的習慣，但是國外的商店大多是**不二價**，但有時你不妨禮貌地問一句：***Can you discount that*？**（能打折嗎？）或許可獲優待，但千萬不可隨便要求不合理的低價。

店　員：***May I help you, sir*？** 需要我幫忙嗎，先生？

　　➪ *Anything I can help you with*？

　　有我能幫忙的地方嗎？

　　➪ *Are you being waited on*？ 您需要服務嗎？

　　➪ *Is there someone helping you*？ 有人幫你忙嗎？

顧　客：Yes, I'm looking for a tie to go with a brown suit.

　　是的，我在找條領帶配棕色西裝。

　　➪ *Could you show me some ties*？

　　你能拿些領帶給我看嗎？

　　➪ *I'd like to see some ties*. 我想看看領帶。

店　員：Certainly, We have a large selection.

　　當然，我們有許多選擇。

　　How about this striped one？ 這條有條紋的如何？

　　It's very nice. 很不錯的。

顧　客：How much is it？多少錢？

➪ *What's the price*？價錢如何？

店　員：It's twenty dollars, sir. 二十元，先生。

顧　客：***Can you discount that***？能打折嗎？

● Notes

go with 搭配　suit〔sut, sjut〕*n.* 西裝

selection〔sə'lɛkʃən〕*n.* 選擇　striped〔straɪpt〕*adj.* 條紋的

discount〔dɪs'kaʊnt〕*v.* 打折

Hint Bank－購物實用語彙

- *sales counter* 結帳員　*department store* 百貨公司
- *shopping mall* 購物中心　*duty-free shop* 免稅店
- *grocery store* 雜貨店　*bargain day* 特價日
- *buy one get one* 買一送一　*gift shop* 禮品店
- *chain store* 連鎖商店　*only one price* 不二價

● 心得筆記欄 ●

CHAPTER 8

辦公室花絮

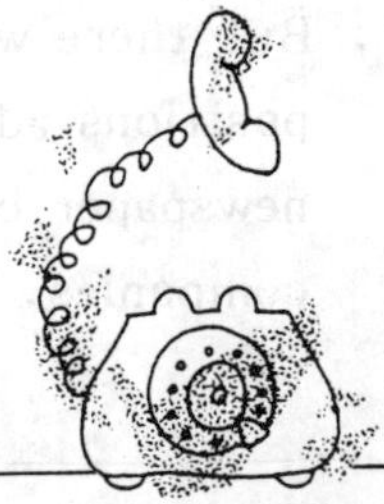

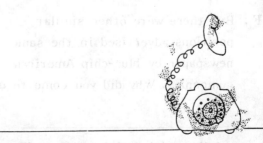

1 Selling oneself in a job interview
求職自我推銷術

《 *Preparation first* 》

求職是每位上班族共有的經驗之一。如何在面試時，作好**自我推銷**，讓別人留下良好的第一印象呢？在前往應徵之前應作好**準備工作**，儘量從各方面收集這家公司的資料，如營業額、在職訓練、創辦人、財務狀況、海外分公司等。最後別忘記告訴主試者 ***I wanted challenge in my career.***（我喜歡有挑戰性的工作。）

詢問應徵目的

F: To start with, can you tell me why you are here today?	外：一開始，請告訴我，您今天為什麼來應徵？
C: I wanted challenge in my career. When I read your ad, I said to myself that ***this is the one opportunity I shouldn't pass up.***	中：我喜歡有挑戰性的工作。當我看見貴公司的廣告時，我就告訴自己，我絕不能錯過這次機會。
F: But there were other similar positions advertised in the same newspaper by blue-chip American companies. Why did you come to us?	外：但是在報上，還有許多績優美商公司所刊的類似求職廣告。為什麼您會到我們這裡來？

**

challenge〔ˈtʃælɪndʒ〕*n*. 挑戰　　blue-chip〔ˈbluˌtʃɪp〕*adj*. 績優的

C : First, you have an impressive growth record. Ever since Mr. Peter Mitchell founded the company 35 years ago, you have doubled in size every five years.

中：第一，貴公司擁有驚人的成長記錄。自從三十五年前，彼得•密契爾先生創建公司以來，貴公司就以每五年成長一倍的速度擴充。

C : Second, marketing is obviously very important for you and ***I will have a great deal to learn from and contribute to your company.*** If possible, I'd like to grow with you.

中：第二，行銷很明顯地對貴公司而言，非常重要，並且我可從貴公司學習到很多事物，而對貴公司有所貢獻。好果可能的話，我希望和貴公司一起成長。

詢問以前的工作

F : Very well. I see you've done your homework, too. You are now with United Butter —— quite a reputable company known for unique point-of-purchase advertising. What is your chief responsibility there?

外：很好。我知道您是有備而來的。您現在任職於聯合奶油公司—— 以獨特的賣場廣告，而聞名的優良公司。您的主要工作是什麼？

**

marketing〔'mɑrkɪtɪŋ〕*n.* 行銷 contribute〔kən'trɪbjʊt〕*v.* 貢獻

point-of-purchase advertising 賣場廣告（＝*POP* 廣告）

C: I've worked there six years since I graduated from college. During the last four years, I've been attending evening classes at a B-school in an MBA program. Well, it took me four years but I've finally gotten the degree.	中：自從我學院畢業後，我就在那裡工作了六年。在最後的四年，我進入B學院的夜間部，修企管碩士的學位。嗯，我花了四年的時間，但最後終於拿到學位。
F: Congratulations	外：恭喜您。
C: Thank you. Two years ago, I was appointed an assistant brand manager responsible for the "Panda" line of margarines. I am also in charge of organizing trade conferences for food distributors held in different parts of the nation almost every month.	中：謝謝您。兩年前，我被任命爲附屬品牌的經理，負責「派達」人造奶油系列的產品。每個月，我亦負責召開全國各地食品經銷商的銷售會議。
C: United Butter is an established and well-managed company and I get to travel around the country. But Panda is not their main product line and maybe it needs to be renamed and repackaged.	中：聯合奶油公司是個制度健全且管理有方的公司，我經常到國內各地出差。但是「派達」並不是他們的主要產品，或許它需要重新命名和包裝。

**

margarine〔'mardʒə,rin,-rın〕*n.* 人造奶油
distributor〔dı'strıbjətɚ〕*n.* 經銷商

說明離職的原因

C: At any rate, I have nothing against United Butter and they've been very nice to me, ***but I'm not sure that I'll be able to make full use of my ability and develop career opportunities there***. Am I going on too much for you?

中：無論如何，我對聯合奶油公司，沒有任何惡意的批評，而且他們對我也不錯，但是我無法確定在那裡，我可以施展所長，開拓職業生涯。我說了太多了嗎？

F: No, not at all. Go right ahead.

外：不，一點也不。請繼續。

C: ***So I had my ear to the ground*** and came across your want ad. I'm very enthusiastic about the job.

中：所以我到處留意，並且發現了貴公司的求才廣告。我對這份工作非常熱中。

說明未來的工作計劃

F: What do you want to be doing in five years' time?

外：在未來的五年中，您希望做些什麼？

C: Honestly, I don't know. Hopefully working for you, but that depends on my value to the company and my job satisfaction.

中：老實說，我並不知道。希望能在貴公司工作，但是需視我對貴公司的價值和我對工作的滿意程度而定。

**

want ad 求才廣告　　enthusiastic〔ɪn,θjuzɪ'æstɪk〕*adj*. 熱誠的；熱中的

C: I don't really know enough about this company to give you an answer. Is that fair enough?	中：我對貴公司的了解尚不夠，無法給您答覆。這樣的回答可以嗎？

自我弱點剖析

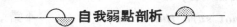

F: Well. What do you think is your biggest weakness?	外：您認爲您最大的弱點是什麼？
C: ***Maybe I'm too aggressive for a Chinese.*** But that will be a big plus when I develop more maturity.	中：作爲一個中國人，我可能太積極了。但是當我更成熟時，那將會非常有利。
C: My greatest strength, on the other hand, is diligence, and realistic and rational thinking habits. ***Most important, I like to deal with people.***	中：另一方面，我最大的力量就是勤奮，和實際及理性的思考習慣。更重要的是，我喜歡和人打交道。
F: Job interviews should be a two-way street. You may ask questions about us, if you have any.	外：面談應該是雙向溝通。如果您有問題，可以對我們提出來。

詢問工作內容待遇

C: Sure. What would my job entail?	外：當然。我的工作內容是什麼？

**

aggressive〔ə'grɛsɪv〕*adj.* 積極的　　plus〔plʌs〕*n.* 利益

F: You would report to me ***with regard to*** all marketing activities for a new line of frozen foods we will be launching here in the fall.

外：你將向我報告有關今年秋季，我們爲新上市冷凍食品系列所展開的行銷活動。

F: During the initial period, it will involve a lot of work and you may be called in on weekends too. ***What salary would you expect to get?***

外：在最初期間，將會牽涉到許多事物，並且週末也要加班。您的希望待遇是多少？

C: Well, I would expect the standard rate of pay at your company for a person with my experience and educational background. Incidentally, I made 6 hundred thousand not including bonus last year.

中：嗯，我希望能夠比照貴公司中，和我同等經驗和學歷的人。順便一提，我去年的年薪是六十萬，包括紅利。

等候通知

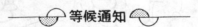

F: OK, I'll be honest with you. You seem to be a go-getter with the right kind of experience and personality and ***you are high on my list.***

外：好的，我對你直言。您似乎是位擁有合適經驗和個性的能手，您是我優先考慮的對象。

** ———

launch〔lɔntʃ, lantʃ〕*v*. 展開　incidentally〔ˌɪnsəˈdɛntəlɪ〕*adv*. 順便一提地
bonus〔ˈbonəs〕*n*. 紅利　go-getter〔ˈgoˈgɛtɚ〕*n*. 能手；活躍進取的人

F: But, as you can imagine, we are still talking to other candidates and so we can't commit ourselves at this stage. Let me assure you that you are definitely ***in the running***, and you will be hearing from us within ten days. Thank you.

外：但是，如您所知的，我們還要和其它應試者面談，所以，我們無法在現階段，給您任何承諾。讓我向您保證，您的勝算很大，我們將在十天內通知您。謝謝您。

**

candidate〔ˈkændə,det, ˈkændədɪt〕*n*. 應試者

commit〔kəˈmɪt〕*v*. 承諾　***in the running*** 勝算很大

Interviewing a job applicant
求職面試

《 *complete consideration* 》

每位主試者都會對**頻換工作**的求職者，產生懷疑，這時你必須提出適當的理由，做完備的考慮，如***My health was quite frail some years ago. But I've never taken a sick leave since I started running five years ago.***（前幾年，我的健康狀況一直不太好。但是，自從五年前，我開始慢跑之後，我就再也沒請過病假了。）

閒聊開場白

F：You seem very fit, Mr. Wang. Do you jog or something?

外：王先生，您看起來非常健康。您有慢跑或作其它運動嗎？

C：Yes, I've been running five kilometers every morning before going to work. Do you do any exercise yourself?

中：是的，我每天早晨上班前，都會慢跑五公里。您本身作運動嗎？

詢問應徵動機

F：***Not really but I should. Now may I ask why you applied for this job?***

外：並不全是，但我是應該作運動。現在，我可以問問你爲什麼來應徵這份工作嗎？

C: Certainly. I read your ad in the paper and was quite excited by the opportunity it seemed to present. You see, I have a good background in marketing.

中：當然可以。我在報上，看到貴公司的廣告，並且爲這份工作的機會感到相當興奮。您看，我對行銷非常有經驗。

更換工作原因

F: You don't seem to have held on to any one job very long, if I may say so. Why did you change jobs so frequently?

外：請恕我直言，您似乎在每個工作都待不久。您爲什麼如此頻繁地更換工作？

C: My health was quite frail some years ago and I couldn't bear the work pressure in some instances. But I've never taken a sick leave since I started running five years ago.

外：前幾年，我的健康狀況一直不太好，有時候無法承受工作上的壓力。但是，自從五年前，我開始慢跑之後，我就再也沒請過病假了。

C: You may also notice that I've been with the present company four and a half years ***and have developed a good knowledge of marketing***. And, if you'd like to see reference letters from my previous companies, I'd be happy to put them in the mail to you later.

外：你可能也注意到，我在目前這家公司已經待了四年半了，而且對於行銷非常在行。如果您願意看看我前任公司的介紹信，我稍後將非常樂意寄給您。

** ———

frail〔frel〕*adj*. 虛弱的　　***sick leave*** 病假

F : No, that won't be necessary. But why do you want to leave your current position?

外：不，那並不需要。但是，你爲什麼要離開目前的職位？

C : I just don't ***get along with*** my boss. There's something in our character that makes us incompatible.

中：我和老板相處不來。我們的個性不合。

待遇問題

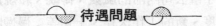

F : May I ask how much you are making now?

外：請問你現在的收入是多少？

C : About 30 thousand.

中：大概三萬元。

F : That's a fairly good salary. I presume you'd want to get at least that much in your new job.

外：那是很高的薪水。我想您會希望，這份工作至少也有這麼多的薪水吧。

C : Hopefully yes, but that's not the only consideration. It also depends on fringe benefits and job security.

中：希望如此，不過那並不是唯一的考慮條件。還要視福利和工作保障而定。

**

incompatible〔,ɪnkəm'pætəbḷ〕*adj*. 不能相容的
presume〔prɪ'zum〕*v*. 假定；認爲 ***fringe benefit*** 福利
security〔sɪ'kjʊrətɪ〕*n*. 保障

The first day on the job
第一天上班

《 *First impression* 》

第一天到公司報到，心情總是非常興奮的。如何和公司的新同事相處融洽就端視你的**第一印象**而定了。在此，建議你**多問問題**，先從了解公司內部的**風氣**、**傳統**、和**規定**開始。再逐一認識工作進度、新的工作伙伴、上司等，慢慢地就可進入情況了。

見面招呼語

F: ***Welcome aboard!*** 外：歡迎你來本公司工作！

C: Thank you. I'm delighted to be working here, Mr. Buchwald. 中：謝謝。我很高興能到這裡來上班，布奇華先生。

F: Call me Buck, will you? My name is Reginald Buchwald but everybody call me Buck. It's easier. 外：叫我布克就可以了，好嗎？我的全名是雷奇納德·布奇華，但是大家都叫我布克。這樣比較方便。

C: ***I would hesitate to*** call you anything but Mr. Buchwald. Isn't it rather disrespectful to make a nickname out of the family name? 中：除了布奇華先生之外，我不好直呼其它的名字。替別人另外取綽號，不是很不禮貌嗎？

**

nick name 綽號

了解公司的風氣

F: Well, President Eisenhower was known as Ike. Everybody in this company all the way up and down the line is called by his or her first name.

外：嗯，艾森豪總統也被暱稱爲艾克。我們公司的上上下下，都是直呼他或她的名字。

F: It's been our tradition ever since the company was small. And don't worry about the disrespect business. OK?

外：從我們公司規模不大時，這就是我們的傳統。不要擔心不禮貌的事了，好嗎？

C: I'll try.

中：我會試試看。

F: Good. But when there are outsiders, like business people from other companies, it might be good practice to address your higher-ups as Mr., Ms. or whatever is appropriate.

外：好。不過，如果有外人在時，如其它公司的商人，最好能稱呼你的上司爲先生，小姐或任何適當的稱謂。

F: ***To the outside world, our custom may be interpreted as a sign of flippancy or lax discipline***. Get it?

外：對外界而言，我們的習慣卻是輕率和紀律鬆弛的表現。懂了嗎？

**

higher-up〔'haɪɚ'ʌp〕*n*. 上司　　appropriate〔ə'proprɪɪt〕*adj*. 適當的
flippancy〔'flɪpənsɪ〕*n*. 輕率；輕浮

C：	Yes, sir.	中：	是的，先生。
F：	(laughing) And don't sir me either. Now I'll show you your private office.	外：	（笑著說）也不要叫我先生。現在，我帶你去看你的私人辦公室。

認識新祕書

C：	Oh, I didn't realize I was getting an office all to myself.	中：	噢，我不知道我可擁有私人辦公室。
F：	Yes, you are. And this is your secretary, Jane Borromeo. She is a Filipina but was born and brought up here and is completely bilingual.	外：	是的，你可以。這是你的祕書，珍・包羅蜜。她是菲律賓人，但在這裡出生和長大，她是個完全能說兩種語言的人。
S：	Hi. How do you do? ***Just holler if you need anything.***	祕：	嗨。你好嗎？如果有任何需要，只要叫我一聲就可以。
C：	Thanks. (to Buchwald) She is a very attractive girl.	中：	謝謝。（對布奇華說）她是個非常迷人的女孩。
F：	And capable, too.	外：	而且也很能幹。
C：	Gee, my nameplate's already on the desk. Everything is so neat.	中：	哇，我的名牌已經放在桌上了。每件東西都很整齊。

**

bilingual〔baɪˈlɪŋgwəl〕*n*. 能說兩種語言的人　　holler〔ˈhɑlɚ〕*v*. 呼叫

成功祕訣

F : ***Feel free to*** drop by my office if you have a question.
外：如果有問題，請不要客氣，隨時到我辦公室來。

C : Even a silly one?
中：即使是個笨問題？

F : How do you know it's silly if you haven't asked?
外：你又沒問，怎麼知道會是個笨問題。

C : My former colleagues told me three secrets of success in foreign-affiliated companies. First, the ability to speak English well.
中：我以前的同事告訴我，要在外商公司成功，有三個祕訣。第一，良好的英語能力。

C : Second, an outgoing and sociable wife. And third, not getting involved in office politics.
中：第二，外向且善於社交的妻子。第三，不要參加公司的政治鬥爭。

F : I agree with the first and the last. You have to be careful when you step into the executive jungle and it's best to stay away from office politics, especially in a big organization like ours.
外：我同意第一點和最後一點。當你踏進爭奪主管的叢林時，必須小心一點，而且最好遠離公司的政治鬥爭，特別是在一個像我們這麼龐大的組織當中。

** ______

colleague〔'kɑlig〕*n.* 同事　***foreign-affiliated company*** 外商公司
outgoing〔'aʊt,goɪŋ〕*adj.* 外向的　jungle〔'dʒʌŋgl̩〕*n.* 叢林；混亂

F: The English ability is helpful but you already have a fine command of it. I'm not so sure about the second.

外：英語能力是有幫助的，但是你的英語已經很好了。我對第二點，並不完全確定。

F: I have a good idea. Why don't you bring your wife to our place for dinner next week? She can compare notes with my wife.

外：我有個好主意。下星期，你爲何不帶你太太到我家來晚餐呢？她可以和我太太交換一下情報。

辦公室規定

C: Thank you, Buck. I'll talk to my wife and find a mutually convenient time. ***Is there anything else I should know before starting to work here?*** Like office regulations?

中：謝謝你，布克。我會和我太太說，並選一個大家方便的時間。在這裡上班之前，還有什麼事情需要知道嗎？像辦公室規定等？

F: You'll get a copy of the manager's manual from our office manager, but LAP is pretty strict about tardiness, clean desks and prompt reports.

外：你會拿到一份我們辦公室經理手册的影印本，但是LAP對於延遲、整理桌面和迅速交報告，有相當嚴厲的規定。

**

manual〔'mænjuəl〕*n.* 手册

pilgrimage〔'pɪlgrəmɪdʒ〕*n.* 朝聖；巡禮

公司副總裁

C : Pardon me, but what's LAP? 中：對不起，但什麼是LAP?

F : That's who, not what. Lawrence A. Pratt, vice president—general manager in Taipei. You've met him before. He goes on a neatness tour of the offices once a month to inspect all the desks.

外：那是人名，不是東西。勞倫斯・波瑞特，在台北的副總裁。你以前見過他。他每個月會作一次桌面清潔巡禮，來檢查所有的桌子。

F : But don't worry, you'll be warned before he goes on his pilgrimage. Oh, here's your program for the week.

外：不過，別擔心，他來之前，我們會先警告你的。噢，這是你這週的計畫表。

工作計劃表

C : A program? 中：計劃表？

F : Yes, you'll spend most of this week talking to different line managers and staff executives, learning about their different functions in the organization. Today you'll be having lunch with our labor relations specialist.

外：是的，你這個星期大部分的時間，都會與不同部門的經理和主管們會談，學習他們在這個組織中的各項功能。今天，你將與我們的勞工關係專家一同午餐。

C : Great! ***I'm impressed with*** your thoroughness.

中：太好了！你的完備介紹令我銘記在心。

4 Participating in a business meeting
參加業務會議

≪ *Staff discussion* ≫

參加業務會議的目的，是要了解各部門的**工作進度**，力求各部門間的妥善**溝通與配合**。並且針對各個問題，共同研討實施的方案。因此事前必須擬出業務**簡報**，提出工作進度和業績。若無法及時完成則可說 ***I'm afraid I'm not yet in a position to give you a complete rundown, as the results are still being tallied.***

Dialogue：*C* ＝ **chairman** 主席　　*B* ＝ **Bob** 鮑伯
M ＝ **Mike** 麥克　　*T* ＝ **Tim** 提姆

主席報告

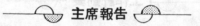

C: Well, gentlemen, you all have a copy of the minutes of the last meeting, so I won't read them. Are there any corrections?

主：嗯，男士們，你們都有上次會議記錄的副本，所以我就不再說了。有任何需要修正的地方嗎？

C: If not, the minutes stand approved. Now, are there any matters arising from them that we need to discuss? Yes, Bob.

主：如果沒有，這份記錄就是通過了。現在，有關於這份記錄，有沒有任何衍生的問題，需要討論的？是的，鮑伯。

契約投標事宜

B：I wish to report that, since our last meeting, we have sent in our bid for a contract to supply electric equipment for ABC Company.

鮑：我要報告的是，自從上次的會議之後，我們就已經送出ABC公司電子設備的契約投標。

B：We're now waiting for the final word, which we expect before the end of this week. ***Prospects are good***, by the way.

鮑：我們正在等候最後的消息，這個星期以前就會有結果。另外，我們的前途非常看好。

回顧檢討

C：Fine. Thank you. Well, then let's go on. The third item on the agenda today is the review of the progress of the "JOIN THE FAN CLUB" campaign. Mike?

主：好的。謝謝你。嗯，讓我們繼續下去。今天議程的第三項是回顧檢討「加入電扇俱樂部」這項活動。麥克？

M：***I'm afraid I'm not yet in a position to give you a complete rundown on the campaign***, as the results are still being tallied.

麥：我恐怕還無法給你完整的活動報告，因爲結果還在核算當中。

**

bid〔bɪd〕*n*. 投標　prospects〔ˈprɑspɛkts〕*n.pl*. 前途；展望
agenda〔əˈdʒɛndə〕*n.pl*. 議程　campaign〔kæmˈpen〕*n*. 活動
rundown〔ˈrʌn,daʊn〕*n*. 摘要報告　tally〔ˈtælɪ〕*v*. 核算

M:	But I'll be able to make an interim report at the next meeting.	麥：	但在下次會議，我可以提出一份暫時報告。
C:	What's your guesstimate?	主：	你的初步估計是什麼？
M:	I'm glad you asked. It's been a real blockbuster. The big air conditioners are out in recent years mainly because of high utility bills and ***our strategy of promoting house fans as the " in " thing with the slogan " JOIN THE FAN CLUB" really caught on and created a sensation in the industry.***	麥：	很高興你問起。這眞是一次大震憾。近年來，大型冷氣機之所以衰退的主要原因，是過高的使用費，我們以「加入電扇俱樂部」這句標語，而發起的倡導使用家庭電扇流行的策略，確實有效，並且在工業界造成轟動。
C:	Three cheers for the planning and sales departments, and also for the advertising department's attention-grabbing ads. We look forward to hearing your report at the next meeting, Mike.	主：	讓我們爲企劃部、銷售部和廣告部引人注意的廣告而喝采。麥克，我們期待著你下次會議的報告。

**

interim〔'ɪntərɪm〕*adj*. 暫時的
blockbuster〔'blɑk,bʌstə〕*n*. (俚) 大型炸彈；震撼
slogan〔'slogən〕*n*. 標語；口號　sensation〔sɛn'seʃən〕*n*. 轟動

C : Now on to the most important subject. Tim, can you explain about this?

主：現在是最重要的主題。提姆，你能解釋這件事嗎？

擬定求才計劃

T : Yes, Mr. Chairman. ***We've always felt the need for*** a systematized recruiting program to attract the graduates going into the job market each year. Up to now, we've hired only five new graduates, but we must have ten to twelve next year if we are to keep growing.

提：是的，主席。我們一直覺得有必要建立系統化的求才計劃，來吸引每年就業市場上的畢業生。到目前爲止，我們只雇用了五名新的畢業生，而如果我們要持續成長，明年一定要雇用十到十二名畢業生。

T : The profile of our target student is somebody with the right frame of mind for a foreign-affiliated company, with a degree in economics, business or law from the group of universities in Taiwan. Preferably he should be able to speak English.

提：我們所需要的人材，是擁有在外商公司工作的正確心態，並且在台灣一流的大學中，主修經濟、貿易或法律的學生。最好還能說英語。

B : Is there such a thing as college recruiting in Taiwan?

鮑：在台灣，有校園求才的活動嗎？

**

profile〔'profaɪl〕*n*, 輪廓；側面像

T : Not in the U.S. sense. Students are allowed to visit corporations and the corporations may start evaluating them—usually through written exams.

提：並不是美國式的。但學生允許到公司參觀，並且由公司開始評估他們—通常是透過筆試的方式。

T : But if we are to start recruiting in earnest, we should plan to produce a brochure and standard application forms.

提：但是，如果我們要愼重地開始徵才，必須計畫印製小册子和標準應徵表格。

C : We need an action plan, too. But do we just wait for the students to come to us?

主：我們也需要行動計劃。但是，我們只要求學生自行前來嗎？

提出建議

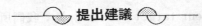

M : ***We should visit placement officers at these universities*** and explain to them about our company and leave copies of our literature.

參：我們應該拜訪各大學的就業輔導部門，向他們介紹我們的公司，並留下我們公司的資料文獻。

**

in earnest 愼重地　　brochure〔broʹʃur〕*n.* 小册子

M： We can also place ads in job guidebooks and employment supplements in newspapers.

麥：我們也可以在求職指南上，刊登廣告，並在報紙上也增刊就業廣告。

結束會議

C： ***I second it.*** Is there any other business? If not, this completes our agenda today. The meeting is adjourned. Our next meeting will be two weeks from today, as usual, that is August 28. ***Thank you everybody for your contributions.***

主：我贊成。還有其它事情嗎？如果沒有，我們就完成今天的議程。現在可以散會。我們下次的會議，將在兩星期之後，就是八月二十八日。謝謝各位的貢獻。

**

supplement〔ˋsʌpləmənt〕*n.* 增刊　　adjourn〔əˋdʒɝn〕*v.* 散會

How to handle a crisis
處理意外事件

≪ *Anti-earthquake* ≫

台灣位在地殼多變動的地帶，因此每年的夏、秋之交是**地震**最頻繁的季節。有鑑於此，有些大樓都設有防備地震的設施，例如台電大樓的防震特殊設計鋼筋及一些外商公司的**顯微膠片**（microfilm）存檔文件。

地震

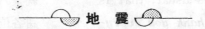

F: Thanks for showing me your well-organized setup here. It has been a very informative and educational tour. Enjoyed it.	外：謝謝你帶我參觀這裡健全的組織體制。這是一次收穫豐富且有教育性的巡視。我非常愉快。
F: Look, is this building swaying? Are we having an earthquake?	外：注意，這棟大樓在搖動嗎？是不是有地震？
C: Yes, ***but this is nothing.*** The tremor will be over in a few seconds.	中：是的，不過這沒什麼。幾秒鐘之後，搖動就會停止了。

**

setup〔'sɛt,ʌp〕*n.* 體制；編制　　earthquake〔'ɝθ,kwek〕*n.* 地震

F: Wow, this is my first earthquake and what a way to feel it—of all places—on the 20th floor of ABC world headquarters! But it does sway. I'm practically seasick!

外：哇，這是我頭一次碰到地震，眞是奇妙的感覺，站在ABC總公司的二十層樓上！但是，卻眞的在搖動。我有些暈船了。

D: Don't worry. This building has been designed to withstand three times the force of the San Fernando Valley Earthquake of 1971.

中：不要擔心。這棟建築物經過特殊設計，可以承受三倍於一九七一年聖范拿多山谷的地震強度。

F: Is that right? Do you have earthquakes frequently in Taipei?

外：是嗎？台北經常發生地震嗎？

C: Yes, it's a problem of the greatest magnitude for us.

中：是的，對我們而言，這是個嚴重的問題。

F: Are you trying to make me feel better or worse?

外：你是在嚇我，還是安慰我？

防範措施

C: Sorry, it was just an accidental pun. ***But the company has taken every conceivable step to minimize loss in contingency.***

中：對不起，只是一個湊巧的雙關語而已。但是,我們公司已採取一切措施,來減低偶發事件的損失。

**

magnitude〔'mægnə,tjud〕*n*. 重要；（地震）（震度）　pun〔pʌn〕*n*. 雙關語
conceivable〔kən'sivəbḷ〕*adj*. 可想像的；可能的
contingency〔kən'tɪndʒənsɪ〕*n*. 偶發事件

F: You sound like a Boy Scout leader upholding the slogan "Be Prepared." I guess it's all over now.

外：聽你這麼說，你好像是一個高舉「萬全準備」標語的童子軍。我想地震停了吧。

F: ***I'm interested in*** knowing what your company has done to prepare for that eventuality.

外：我有興趣了解一下貴公司，對突發事件所做的萬全準備。

顯微膠片存檔文件

C: The worst that could happen is the complete destruction of this building. ***With the destruction of the headquarters building***, the huge communication network would crumble, and we'd lose millions of info files, contracts and other documents.

中：在最糟的情況下，整棟建築物有倒塌的危險。總公司一倒塌，大型的通訊網就會瓦解，我們也會損失上百萬的資料檔案，契約和其它文件。

C: All key documents, including contracts, have been microfilmed, and they are kept in duplicate, one set in the basement of this building and another in Pittsburgh.

中：所有重要文件，包括契約，都被製成顯微膠片，並且複製二份，一份放在這棟大樓的地下室，一份放在匹玆堡的公司。

**

eventuality〔ɪ,vɛntʃʊ'ælətɪ〕*n*. 突發事件；可能發生的事件；可能性
crumble〔'krʌmbḷ〕*v*. 瓦解；崩潰　microfilm〔'maɪkrə,fɪlm〕*v*. 製成顯微膠片

F: So you are well protected!
外:所以,你們是防護周全的!

C: I may also add that we have a list of amateur radio operators among our employees, who would offer help in emergency communications.
中:我再補充一點,我們的員工中,有一組業餘的無線電操作員,可以在緊急通訊時,予以協助。

危機處理研討會

F: It seems the Chinese are capable of making such thorough plans. If you should visit New York, I'll show you our crisis management seminar. That's where we train our managers to be better corporate spokespersons ***through simulated crisis situations and role playing.***
外:中國人似乎對策劃完整的計劃,很有一套。如果你來紐約,我將帶你參觀我們的危機處理研討會。這是我們訓練經理人員,透過模擬危機狀況和角色扮演,而成爲出色的企業代表人。

C: ***That sounds very exciting.*** In fact, I'll be in New York in September, and I'd very much like to observe one.
中:聽起來很刺激。事實上,我九月將去紐約,我非常樂意去觀摩一下。

F: ***Be my guest.*** Write to me before you come and I'll have all the necessary arrangements made for you.
外:請來當我的客人。你來之前,請寫信給我,我將爲你安排所有必要的約會。

**

amateur〔'æmə,tʃʊr, -,tʊr〕*adj*. 業餘的

Over lunch
午餐時間

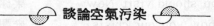

《 ***Business lunch*** 》

歐美人士一般喜歡利用**午餐時間**來進行商業會談或推銷，稱之爲 ***business lunch*** 。而晚餐的時間，則爲純粹社交的招待，通常都不談生意上的話題。靈活地運用商業午餐來進行洽談，在輕鬆愉快的氣氛中，完成交易，是善用時間的最佳說明。

談論空氣污染

F: Such a nice view from here. ***Almost unbelievable that you have smog in this city.***

外：從這裡遠眺，景緻眞好。簡直不敢相信城中的煙霧這麼重。

C: It's not so bad after a long weekend, but we have pretty dense smog in the winter. The white smog in summer is nasty, too.

中：在周末之後，情形不會那麼嚴重，但在冬天，煙霧眞的很濃。夏天白色煙霧也很污穢。

談論台北進步快速

F: This is my first visit since 1946. This area was almost all flat in those days. Now it's all skyscrapers.

外：自從一九四六年以來，這是我第一次到這裡來。那時候，這一區還都是平房。沒有摩天大樓。

C：If you come back in five years, you probably won't recognize this either. They are going to tear down that whole neighborhood down there as part of an urban renewal.

中：假如你五年後，再回來，你可能也不認得這一區了。他們即將把那裡的整個地區夷平，規劃爲都市重建的一部分。

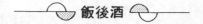

飯後酒

F：Do you want a drink?

外：要來杯酒嗎？

C：Are you having one?

中：你要喝嗎？

F：I think I'll have a Bloody Mary.

外：我想來杯血腥瑪麗。

C：***Then I'll go for a*** Campari soda. Let me get a waiter.

中：那麼，我來杯康巴里蘇打水。我來叫侍者。

談論期票

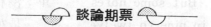

F：I didn't quite understand some of the conversation you were having earlier in the office. What was the thing about the promissory notes?

外：我不太了解早先你們在辦公室的談話。什麼是期票呢？

**

nasty〔'næstɪ〕*adj*. 汚穢的

skyscraper〔'skaɪ,skrepɚ〕*n*. 摩天大樓

promissory note 期票

C: It's typical of some large Taiwan companies to pay their suppliers in promissory notes. One of our new clients offered to pay us half in promissory notes, and half in barter tickets and we are trying to fight them off.

中：台灣的公司，通常會以期票支付給供應商。我們一位新客戶，提出一半期票，一半現金的支付方式，而我們正在抵制他們。

F: How does a promissory note work?

外：期票是如何運用？

C: It is a written promise to pay a designated amount at a certain future time — in their case, in six months.

中：那是一張標明應付款項，及在未來的某一時間付款的承諾書 —— 在他們公司的情形，是六個月後。

F: Six months! At no interest?

外：六個月後！沒有利息嗎？

C: No interest. But some notes are payable in nine to twelve months.

中：沒有利息。但有些期票是在九到十二個月內付款。

F: We can't afford to work like that. ***It'll have a terrible effect on our cash flow.*** We're not a bank. Won't they agree to pay in cash?

外：我們就無法那麼做。那會嚴重地影響我們的現金周轉。我們不是銀行。他們不同意付現金嗎？

C: Don't know yet.

中：還不知道。

** ———

designate〔'dɛzɪg,net〕*v*. 標明；指出

接受充電訓練

F: ***Looks like everybody is keeping you busy.*** It's been some time since you were last in the States and I reckon that ***it's time you took refresher training in the New York office.***

外：好像每個人都少不了你似的。從你上次來美國，已經隔了一段時間，我認爲該是你到紐約，接受充電訓練的時候了。

C: Thank you very much, Mr. Christian.

中：謝謝你，克里斯坦先生。

單身赴任？

F: Do you want to bring your wife along?

外：你想帶你太太一同前來嗎？

C: I'd like to, but I'm not sure we can afford it.

中：我是想，但是，我不確定是否付得起。

F: As we say in the States, if you bring your wife, ***it's twice as expensive but half the fun.*** Right? ***But seriously,*** if she could manage to get away, she could stay with us while you attend the seminar.

外：在美國，假如你帶太太前去，費用會增加，但樂趣會減半。對嗎？但說正經的，如果她要前來，當你去開會時，她可以和我們在一起。

C: Gee, ***that's very considerate of you.*** I'm sure my wife will appreciate it.

中：喔，你眞是體貼。我太太一定會非常感謝你的。

F : Good. Talk to her and let me know later. 外：好。請告訴她，稍後再通知我。

閒聊房地產

F : I heard you bought a new house. 外：我聽說你買了新房子。

C : Well, it's a very small one. It's so small we even use condensed milk and concentrated juice. 中：是的，一棟小房子。小到我們必需喝濃縮牛奶和壓縮果汁。

F : (laughing) You've got to be kidding. ***Is housing expensive in Taiwan?*** 外：（笑著說）你在開玩笑。台灣的房子很貴嗎？

C : ***Real estate prices are just astronomical in big cities.*** It takes me exactly 60 minutes to get to work, which is not bad for Taipei. 中：在大城市中的房地產價格，簡直是天文數字。我每天要花一個鐘頭通勤上班，在台北還不算太壞。

F : Can the average worker afford to buy a house? 外：一般的勞工可以買得起房子嗎？

C : Not really. Many large companies have ***subsidized housing***, though, where the occupants pay a nominal monthly rent of, say, NT$2500 or so. 中：不完全買得起。然而許多大企業公司設有員工補助宿舍，每個月只要名義上付大約新台幣二千五百元就夠了。

**

reckon〔'rɛkən〕*v*. 認爲；想　***refresher training*** 充電訓練

real estate 房地產；不動產　astronomical〔,æstrə'nɑmɪkḷ〕*adj*. 天文數字的

occupant〔'ɑkjəpənt〕*n*. 居住者　nominal〔'nɑmənḷ〕*adj*. 名義上的；極少的

Working for a female boss
女性主管

《 *Career woman* 》

隨著**職業婦女**（ ***career woman*** ）的增加，**女性主管**（ ***female boss*** ）的比率也越來越高。如果妳也是一位女性主管，不妨對部屬說： ***All I'm asking for is that you look at our working relationship with an open mind.*** （我所要求的是，請你們以開放的心胸，來看待我們的工作關係。）

Dialogue： *J* = **Janny** 珍妮　　*M* = **Mike** 麥克

生命中的兩個女人

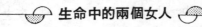

J： Do you think you may be a bit biased against women?

珍：你是否對女性有些偏見？

M： I'm not sure if it's a bias, but ***I'm just uncomfortable working for a female boss. Looks as though two women dominate my life.***

麥：我不確定那是否是偏見。但是爲女性主管工作，總是令我不舒服。看起來，似乎是讓兩個女人，來支配我的一生。

** ————————————

bias〔'baɪəs〕 *n.* 偏見；成見

dominate〔'dɑmə,net〕 *v.* 支配；控制

J: So you're saying that you wouldn't really like to work for a supervisor because she is a woman.

珍：所以，你是說你確實不願意有個女性主管，就是因爲她是個女人。

M: That sounds awful, doesn't it?

麥：聽起來很可怕，不是嗎?

J: ***I think it's an injustice to her.*** It so happens that I have more responsibility in this company than you do. And it's only incidental that I am a woman.

珍：我認爲這對她不公平。我在公司中的職責，比你們都重。而且，只是碰巧我是個女人。

M: You're so right, but if it is a bias — as you suspect it is— I probably won't be able to change that attitude overnight.

麥：你是對的，但是，如果這就是你所說的偏見，一夜之間，我還無法改變那種態度。

開放的心胸

J: I understand that. But all I'm asking for is that you look at our working relationship ***with an open mind. There should be no psychological barrier between us*** just because I'm a woman.

珍：我了解。但我所要求的是，請你以開放的心胸來看待我們的工作關係。不能只是因爲我是個女人，我們彼此就存有心理障礙。

**

awful〔'ɔful〕*adj.* 可怕的
incidental〔,ɪnsə'dɛntl̩〕*adj.* 碰巧的；偶發的
psychological barrier 心理障礙

M: What about in the States? A lot of women work there. Is there complete equality for both sexes?

麥:美國的情形如何?在美國,有很多女性就業者。兩性之間,擁有完全的平等嗎?

兩性之間的平等

J: The federal government has passed laws ***against discrimination by sex, age, race, religion and other factors.***

珍:聯邦政府已經通過反對性別、年齡、種族、宗教和其它因素的歧視法案。

J: If a woman employee feels that she is being unfairly treated because of her sex, she can ***bring the matter to court.***

珍:如果一位女性職員,覺得自己因爲性別原因,而受到差別待遇,她可以上訴法院。

M: I see. Are there a lot of female managers?

麥:我懂了。有很多女性管理人員嗎?

**

equality〔ɪ'kwɑlətɪ〕*n.* 平等

discrimination〔dɪ,skrɪmə'neʃən〕*n.* 歧視

女性管理人員

J: Now about 41 percent of the labor force in America are women. But only about five percent of managerial posts are filled by women.

珍：現在，美國勞工總數的百分之四十一都是女性。但大約只有百分之五的管理人員是女性。

M: Don't women have a much higher ***turnover rate*** than men?

麥：女性的離職率不是比男性高嗎？

J: The rate is only slightly higher for women. Statistics say that men tend to take longer and more frequent sick leaves than women. There are a lot of these myths about women that need to be ***cleared up***, though.

珍：只是稍微高了一些。統計上說，男性有比女性更常請病假和長假的傾向。雖然有許多這類有關女性的虛構事件，但卻必須被澄清。

**

turnover rate 離職率　statistics〔stə'tɪstɪks〕*n*. 統計
myth〔mɪθ〕*n*. 虛構事件；神話

CHAPTER 9

充電實用資訊篇

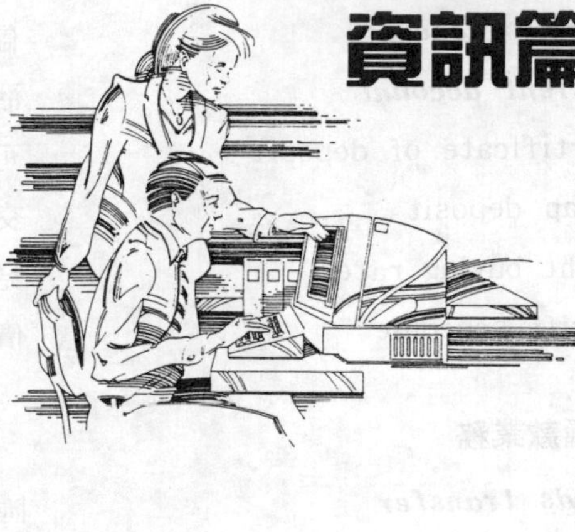

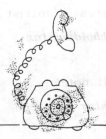

Part 1 銀行股市用語

◉ 窗口業務

teller [ˈtɛlɚ] *n.*	銀行出納員
depositor [dɪˈpɑzɪtɚ] *n.*	存款者
demand deposit	可隨時要求提出的存款
time deposit	定期儲金
savings account	儲金帳戶
current account	活期存款
certificate of deposit	可轉讓定期儲金證明書
swap deposit	交換存款
sight buying rate	見票即付匯票牌價
tariff schedule	價目表

◉ 匯款業務

funds transfer	匯送專款
our account	本方結帳
their account	對方結帳
traveller's check	旅遊支票
statement of account	帳戶清單
interest [ˈɪntrɪst] *n.*	利息
withholding tax	雇主替政府從受雇者薪水中扣繳的所得稅
debit note	付款通知
counter rate	對顧客的匯兌利率

cover ['kʌvɚ] *n.*	負債準備金
$ ***clearing*** ['klɪrɪŋ] *n.*	票據結算
demand draft	銀行匯款支票
debit advice	付款通知

◉貸款業務

borrower ['bɑroɚ] *n.*	借入者
lender ['lɛndɚ] *n.*	貸方
rollover ['rol,ovɚ] *n.*	借款轉期
credit crunch	信用緊縮
impact loan	沒有開銷限制的外匯貸款
term loan	長期貸款
project loan	計畫貸款
multicurrency loan	多國通貨借款
syndicated loan	企業協調融資
swap loan	買賣借款
promissory note	期票
bill of exchange	匯票
letter of hypothecation	擔保狀
commitment fee	買賣契約手續費
tenor ['tɛnɚ] *n.*	期限
grace period	支付延期期間
floating interest rate	流動利率
fixed interest rate	固定利率
banker's acceptance	銀行承兌票據
collateral security	附屬擔保物

prime rate	最優惠利率
lifting charge	受理手續費
letter of guarantee	保證書
clean loan	無擔保融資
secured loan	有擔保融資
bills discount	票據貼現

◉ **其它業務**

export bill	出口票據
sight bill	見票即付票據
usance bill	有票據期限的票據
mail interest	郵政利率
shippers' usance	輸出業者支付的票據利息
buyers' usance	輸入業者支付的票據利息
clean credit	銀行發行的信用狀
reimbursement 〔,riɪm'bɜsmənt〕*n.*	償還；退款
confirmed L/C	保兌信用狀
advising bank	通知銀行
restricted L/C	限制信用狀
revolving L/C	回轉信用狀
L/C without recourse	不接受追索權的信用狀
L/C with recourse	接受追索權的信用狀
trust receipt	輸入擔保貨物證明書
transshipment 〔træns'ʃɪpmənt〕*n.*	轉運他船
documents against payment	收到文件後付款
documents against acceptance	收到文件後承兌

bond 〔bɑnd〕*n.*	保證書
drawer 〔'drɔɚ〕*n.*	開票人
drawee 〔drɔ'i〕*n.*	受票人
endorsement 〔ɪn'dɔrsmənt〕*n.*	背書
correspondent bank	通匯銀行
spot deal	當場交易
forward contract	期貨契約
swap deal	交換買賣
outright deal	現金買賣
swap rate	交換買賣的利率
overbought position	買進外匯的價格超出賣出的價格
oversold position	賣出外匯的價格超出買進的價格
square position	匯票的買進賣出收支平衡
arbitrage 〔'ɑrbətrɪdʒ〕*n.*	套滙
marry 〔'mærɪ〕*n.*	外滙的收支相抵
speculation 〔,spɛkjə'leʃən〕*n.*	投機買賣
exchange risk	滙兌風險
hedge 〔hɛdʒ〕*v.*	兩方下注
rate risk	匯率變動風險
cross rate	匯兌率
value date	期限
maturity date	期滿日期
exchange broker	外匯仲介者
money market	短期金融市場
funding 〔'fʌndɪŋ〕*n.*	週轉資金
interest swap	利息交換

currency swap	本金及利息的交換
hard currency	强勢貨幣
soft currency	弱勢貨幣
tax haven	實行優待稅制的國家或地區
Eurocurrency [ˈjʊrə,kɝənsɪ] *n.*	歐洲貨幣
Eurodollar [ˈjʊrə,dɑlɚ] *n.*	歐洲美元
European Monetary System	歐洲金融系統
European Currency Unit	歐洲貨幣單位
International Monetary Market	國際金融市場
World Bank	世界銀行
fixed exchange rate system	固定匯率系統
floating exchange rate system	流動匯率系統
devaluation [,divæljʊˈeʃən] *n.*	貶値
external debt	外債
debt service ratio	債務負擔率
moratorium [,mɔrəˈtorɪəm] *n.*	延期償付令
deregulation [di,rɛgjəˈleʃən] *n.*	取消管制
Glass-Steagall Act	1933年施行的美國銀行法，禁止銀行兼營證券業務
McFadden Act	1927年施行的美國銀行法，禁止越州進行州際銀行業務
crowding out	為了貼補財政赤字而緊縮民間所需的資金
reciprocity [,rɛsəˈprɑsətɪ] *n.*	商業互惠
bank-holding company	銀行持股公司

◉股市用語

stock [ˈstɑk] *n.*	公債；股票
share [ʃɛr] *n.*	股份；股權
stock certificate	公債證書
common stock	普通股
preferred stock	優良股
capital stock	（公司的）股票總額
capitalization [ˈkæpɪtələˈzeʃən] *n.*	資本額的估計
issued stock	發行股票
authorized stock	核定股票
equity [ˈɛkwətɪ] *n.*	持股
par [pɑr] *n.*	票面價值
no-par stock	無票面額的股票
shareholder [ˈʃɛr,holdɚ] *n.*	股東
transfer agent	過戶代理人
beneficial owner	受益人
dividend [ˈdɪvə,dɛnd] *n.*	股息
split [splɪt] *n.*	分割股票
treasury stock	公司買自己公司的股票
blue chip	優良股
glamour stock	魅力股（指後勁看好的股票）
growth stock	成長股
watered stock	虛報資產的公司股票
board [bord, bɔrd] *n.*	證券交易所
floor [flor, flɔr] *n.*	（交易所內的）市場
opening price	開盤

closing price	收盤
round lot	最低交易單位
income gain	股利收入
extra dividend	額外股利
bonus stock	紅股
guarantee stock	保利股
cash dividend	現金配股
principal transaction	非透過仲介公司交易
agency transaction	委託（仲介公司）交易
bear market	股市疲乏
bull market	股市强勁
churning ['tʃɝnɪŋ] *n.*	過份地勸顧客買賣股票
corner ['kɔrnɚ] *n.*	壟斷市場
manipulation [mə,nɪpjʊ'leʃən] *n.*	操縱市場
rally ['rælɪ] *n.*	景氣恢復
stabilization [,stebələ'zeʃən] *n.*	幣值的穩定
wash sale	假裝買賣
grey market	新發行證券的預約買賣市場
auction market	拍賣市場
futures market	期貨市場
financial futures market	金融期貨市場
back office	事務部
broker ['brokɚ] *n.*	經紀人；掮客
dealer ['dilɚ] *n.*	證券交易者
discretionary order	自由裁量訂購
not held order	大量買進，使牌價崩潰

margin buying	信用交易買進
margin agreement	信用交易承諾書
margin requirement	信用交易必要的保證金
margin call	追加保證金要求
short [ʃɔrt] *n.*	買空賣空的人(投機分子)
cash sale	現金買賣
margin account	信用交易帳戶
custodian account	證券保管帳戶
confirmation [ˌkɑnfəˈmeʃən] *n.*	買賣報告書
buy in	大批買進
due bill	借用證
capital gain	買賣股票的獲利
capital loss	買賣股票的虧損
paper profit	紙上獲利(未實現的)
profit taking	套利
price appreciation	增值
bond [bɑnd] *n.*	股票;公債
debenture [dɪˈbɛntʃɚ] *n.*	無擔保公司債
straight bond	普通債券
convertible bond	可抵換借貸的債券
government bond	政府公債
municipal bond	地方公債
corporate bond	公司債券
notes [nots] *n.pl.*	中期債券
coupon bond	定期付利的債券
Eurobond [ˈjʊrəˌbɑnd] *n.*	歐洲債券

zero-coupon bond	無利息債券
deep discount bond	低率債券
partly paid bond	分期償付債券
floating rate note	變動利率債券
mortgage bond	抵押債券
commercial paper	短期商業支票
bearer bond	不記名債券
registered bond	記名債券
due date	到期日期
face value	票面額
maturity [mə'tjʊrətɪ] *n.*	期滿
debt financing	發行債券所進行的資金調度
equity financing	發行股票所進行的資金調度
new issue	開始發行新證券
issue price	發行價格
hot issue	發行額度上漲的證券
underwriter ['ʌndɚ,raɪtɚ] *n.*	證券承購人
balanced fund	分散投資股票
offshore fund	爲了減低稅金而做的股票投資
trustee [trʌs'ti] *n.*	被信託人
closed-end fund	封閉式信託基金
open-end fund	開放式信託基金
sinking fund	減債基金
investment trust	投資信託
point [pɔɪnt] *n.*	（稱呼股票行情的）檔
amortize ['æmɚ,taɪz] *v.*	分期償清

Part 2 台北知名觀光飯店

• Grand / 圓山
1 Chungshan N. Rd., Sec.4, Taipei
台北市中山北路4段1號
TEL: (02) 596-5565

• Hilton / 希爾頓
38 Chunghsiao W. Rd. Sec.1, Taipei
台北市忠孝西路1段38號
TEL: (02) 311-5151

• Asiaworld Plaza Hotel / 環亞
100, Tunhwa N. Rd., Taipei
台北市敦化北路100號
TEL: (02) 715-0077

• Ambassador / 國賓
63 Chungshan N. Rd., Sec. 2, Taipei
台北市中山北路2段63號
TEL: (02) 551-1111

• Howard Plaza / 福華
160 Jenai Rd., Sec. 3, Taipei
台北市仁愛路3段160號
TEL: (02) 700-2323

• Mandarin / 中泰
166 Tunhwa N. Rd., Taipei
台北市敦化北路166號
TEL: (02) 712-1201

• Ritz / 亞都
155 Minchuan E. Rd., Taipei
台北市民權東路155號
TEL: (02) 597-1234

• Lai Lai Sheraton / 來來
12 Chunghsiao E. Rd., Sec. 1, Taipei
台北市忠孝東路1段12號
TEL: (02) 321-5511

• Brother / 兄弟
255 Nanking E. Rd., Sec. 3, Taipei
台北市南京東路3段255號
TEL: (02) 712-3456

• Majestic / 美琪
2 Minchuan E. Rd., Taipei
台北市民權東路2號
TEL: (02) 581-7111

- Rebar / 力霸
  32 Nanking E. Rd., Sec.5,
  台北市南京東路 5 段 32 號
  TEL: (02) 763-5656

- Astar / 亞士都
  98 Linshen N. Rd., Taipei
  台北市林森北路 98 號
  TEL: (02) 551-3131

- Leofoo / 六福
  168 Changchun Rd., Taipei
  台北市長春路 168 號
  TEL: (02) 581-3111

- Gloria / 華泰
  369 Linshen N. Rd., Taipei
  台北市林森北路 369 號
  TEL: (02) 581-8111

- Taipei Miramar / 美麗華
  420 Minchuan E. Rd., Taipei
  台北市民權東路 420 號
  TEL: (02) 505-3456

- Grand Hyatt Hotel / 凱悅
  2 Sung Shou Rd. Taipei
  台北市松壽路 2 號
  TEL: (02) 720-1234

- The Sherwood Hotel-Taipei / 西華
  637 Ming Sheng East Rd. Taipei
  台北市民生東路 637 號
  TEL: (02) 718-1188

- San Polo / 三普
  172 Chunghsiao E. Rd., Sec. 4, Taipei
  台北市忠孝東路 4 段 172 號
  TEL: (02) 772-2121

- Taipei Fortuna / 富都
  122 Chungshan N. Rd., Sec. 2, Taipei
  台北市中山北路 2 段 122 號
  TEL: (02) 563-1111

- Royal / 老爺
  37-1 Chungshan N. Rd., Sec. 2, Taipei
  台北市中山北路 2 段 37-1 號
  TEL: (02) 542-3266

- President / 統一
  9 Tehwei St., Taipei
  台北市德惠街 9 號
  TEL: (02) 595-1251

- The Regent of Taipei / 麗晶
  41 Chungshan N. Rd., Sec. 2, Taipei
  台北市中山北路 2 段 41 號
  TEL: (02) 523-8000

Part 8 熱門話題1

愛滋病

AIDS

Horrible disease

二十世紀的黑死病── AIDS，已由美洲登陸台灣了！這種人人聞之色變的疾病，真的會經由空氣而傳染嗎？

Dialogue:

A: ***I hear that*** the company is sending you to San Francisco next month. 我聽說下個月，公司將派你去舊金山。

B: Yes, I'll be working there for two months and then I'll be back. I'm excited.
是的，我將在那裡工作兩個月，然後再回來。我非常興奮。

B: Do you know anything about San Francisco?
你知道任何有關舊金山的事嗎？

A: A little. 知道一些。

B: This city ***is known for*** the legalized homosexuals. I think it must be a terrible city because of AIDS.
這座城市以合法同性戀而聞名。我想因爲愛滋病的原故，那一定是個可怕的城市。

A: ***AIDS could be transmitted by blood as far as the experts can tell.*** However, people who get the disease usually come

** legalized 〔'ligḷ,aɪzd〕 *adj.* 予以合法化的

from " high risk groups ", such as homosexuals or intravenous drug users. You can't get AIDS just by going to San Francisco. Besides, AIDS is everywhere. Even in Taiwan.
專家證明，愛滋病可經由血液傳染。然而，患病者通常是來自「高危險群」，像同性戀者或藥物靜脈注射者。你只是到舊金山市，不會得愛滋病的。而且，愛滋病到處都有。連台灣也有。

B: Oh yes, I remember. There was a university student who got the disease last year. He was a homosexual I believe.
噢，對了，我記起來了。去年，有一位大學生罹患愛滋病。我相信他是同性戀者。

A: You see, he comes from a " high risk group ". ***As long as you stay away from*** things that " high risk group " people do, then your chances of getting AIDS are unlikely.
你看，他就是來自「高危險群」。只要你遠離「高危險群」所做的事，那麼，你就不可能有機會得到愛滋病。

B: ***I guess I should know much more about it.***
我想我應該對愛滋病多了解一些。

A: Yes, you should. It could save your life. AIDS is a terrible way to die.
是的，你應該如此。這將會保障你生命的安全。愛滋病是種可怕的死亡方式。

** transmit〔træns'mɪt〕*v*. 傳染　***high risk group*** 高危險群
intravenous〔,ɪntrə'vinəs〕*adj*. 靜脈注射的
as long as 只要　unlikely〔ʌn'laɪklɪ〕*adj*. 不可能的

Part 8 熱門話題2

頂克族

DINK

Double Income No Kids

在台灣，頂克族（DINK）有越來越多的趨勢。以下是一對外國夫婦和李先生的對話。

Dialogue:

A: Hello, Mr. Lee. Nice to see you again.
嗨，李先生。很高興再次見到你。

C: Hello, John. I didn't know you were back in Taiwan. It's good to see you too! ***How have you been?***
嗨，約翰。我不知道你已經回到台灣了。我也很高興見到你。近來可好？

A: Well, I got married last year. This is my wife Jenny.
嗯，我去年剛結婚。這是內人珍妮。

B: ***Pleased to make your acquaintance***, Mr. Lee.
李先生，很高興認識你。

A: Oh, ***the pleasure is mine***. Is this your first time to Taiwan? 噢，這是我的榮幸。這是妳第一次到台灣來嗎？

** acquaintance〔ə'kwentəns〕*n*. 熟識

B: No, I've been here for years. I work here at the World Trade Center.

不，我在這裡好幾年了。我在世貿中心工作。

A: Yes, she and I both have full time jobs. We are ***what they call*** in the U.S. " a Double Income No Kids Family ", or " DINK Family ".

是的，我和內人都有全職的工作。我們就是美國人所謂的「雙收入無小孩家庭」或「頂克家庭」。

C: Well, in this day and age, it's important to build a strong household before bringing new life into it. Say, doesn't the word " dink " have another meaning?

嗯，在今天這個時代，要迎接新生命誕生之前，先建立穩固的家庭是很重要的。對了，「dink」這個字，沒有別的意思嗎？

A: Two actually. One is an American slang that's not very nice, and the other is from a Scottish word meaning well dressed. 事實上，有兩個意思。一個是個美國俚語，但意思不佳，另外一個意思是源於蘇格蘭字，有穿著得體之意。

** household〔'haus,hold〕 *n*. 家庭
Scottish〔'skatɪʃ〕 *adj*. 蘇格蘭的

Part 3 熱門話題3

大衆捷運系統

Mass Rapid Transit System

Don't be late

每天趕公車上班，實在是上班族最頭痛的事。因此，大衆捷運系統到底何時會完工呢？這更是你我的熱門話題。

Dialogue:

A: Bob, are you late again? This is the fourth time in two weeks. Mr. Lin is going to be angry with you.
鮑伯，你又遲到了嗎？這是你兩個星期以來，第四次遲到了。林先生將會對你不滿的。

B: I know, but ***I can't help it. The traffic is what held me up.*** I have to come all the way from Shih Lin every morning. Sometimes it takes over an hour.
我知道，但是我實在沒辦法。都是交通問題惹的禍。我每天早上要從士林趕來上班。有時候要花上一個多小時。

A: I know. I have to ***come all the way from*** Tien Mu myself. I wake up at 5:30 every morning just to get here on time. I can't wait until they finish the MRTS.
我知道。我每天早上，五點半就起床，也只能準時從天母到達這裡。我可不能等到大衆捷運系統完工。

** traffic〔'træfɪk〕*n.* 交通

B: Is that the subway system? 是地下鐵嗎？

A: Yes, it's the Mass Rapid Transit System.
是的，那是大衆捷運系統。

B: When is it supposed to be completed?
那何時可以完工呢？

A: Unfortunately, ***not until the end of the century.***
很不幸地，要等到本世紀末。

B: That's a long wait. Why didn't they start working on it earlier? Taipei needs it now, not ten years from now.
那要等好久。爲什麼他們不早點做呢？台北現在就需要它，而不是在十年以後。

A: Actually, some far-sighted politicians began studies for a mass transit system over twenty years ago. The problem has been, and still is, the refusal of some landowners to sell their land. But it's being forced through now.
事實上，一些有遠見的政界人士，早在二十年前就研究過大衆捷運系統了。問題是，有些地主不願意出售土地。但是現在已經被解決了。

B: But what can I do until they finish it?
但是在完工之前，我該怎麼辦呢？

A: Start setting your alarm clock for 5:30 A.M.
開始將鬧鐘撥到五點半。

** subway〔'sʌb,we〕*n.* 地下鐵路　complete〔kəm'plit〕*v.* 完工
politician〔,pɑlə'tɪʃən〕*n.* 政治家

Part 8 熱門話題4

罷工

Strike

Sit-down Strike

最近，台灣掀起一陣自力救濟的風潮。公車、客運、雞農的遊行罷工更是層出不窮，成為人們茶餘飯後的話題。

Dialogue:

A：Mr. Chen, will the transportation strike affect our company？陳先生，運輸罷工將會影響公司嗎？

B：It shouldn't affect us too much in the short term, but if it continues we might have to find other means to ship our products. 在短期內應該不會，但是假如罷工持續下去，我們就必須找其它的方法來運送貨物。

A：I saw on the news last night that the workers were all outside of the Transportation Ministry in a ***sit down strike***. There were ***hundreds of*** police there too!
我昨天晚上看報紙上說，工人們在交通部外面靜坐罷工。當場還有上百位警察呢！

** transportation〔,trænspə'teʃən〕*n*. 運輸
affect〔ə'fɛkt〕*v*. 影響　　continue〔kən'tɪnjʊ〕*v*. 持續；繼續
Transportation Ministry 交通部

B : Yes, they're worried that it might ***turn into a riot***. They had some trouble when some scabs tried to cross the picket line. 是的，他們擔心罷工會演變爲暴動。當一些流氓試圖通過警戒線時，他們有些麻煩。

A : ***When did they walk off of the job***?
他們什麼時候開始罷工的？

B : They ***went on strike*** two days ago. But ***the writing was on the wall*** for weeks. I knew that the stike was imminent, so we prepared for the worst. As I said, we should be all right for now.
他們兩天前開始罷工。但是在幾星期以前，就有醞釀的前兆了。我知道罷工是很迫切的，所以我們做了最壞的打算。如我所說，到目前爲止，我們都還好。

A : What are the workers demanding? 工人們要求什麼呢？

B : They want a pay raise and more vacation time — basically a whole new contract. I think the management is going to ***meet the union half-way*** on their demands. Hopefully it will be over soon.
他們要求加薪，和更多的休假——基本上是要求一個新合約。我想有關單位將會對工會的要求妥協。希望罷工很快就能結束。

** riot〔'raɪət〕*n*. 暴動　scab〔skæb〕*n*. 流氓；無賴
picket line 警戒線　***walk off*** 退出（以示抗議）
writing on the wall 災難的前兆　imminent〔'ɪmənənt〕*adj*. 迫切的
meet a person half-way 與人妥協

Part 8 熱門話題5

算命

Fortune Telling

Astrology

根據統計，知識水準越高的人，越有相信算命的趨勢。在瞬息萬變的商場上，工商人士迷信風水者，更是大有人在。相信許多老外一定對這種現象大為不解。

Dialogue：

A：I'm going to ***take a chance*** on this stock option. Do you think I should consult a fortune teller first ? There are many here in Taiwan.

我將在股票上碰碰運氣。你想我是不是該先請教算命先生？在台灣有很多算命先生。

B：***It's probably a good idea.*** 這或許是個好主意。

A：I was just joking. 我只是開玩笑的。

B：I wasn't. I'm serious. You would be surprised at how accurate my fortune teller is. She uses astrology, palm reading, and face reading. I would go to her if I was making a big financial decision. 我可不是。我是認眞的。你會驚訝，算命先生的話是那麼準確靈驗。她會看占星術、手相、和面相。如果我要做重大的財務決定時，我會先去找她。

** option〔'ɑpʃən〕*n.* 選擇　　consult〔kən'sʌlt〕*v.* 求教；磋商
fortune teller 算命先生　　accurate〔'ækjərɪt〕*adj.* 準確；靈驗

A: Bob, I'm truly surprised that you believe in that stuff. It's just a lot of mumbo jumbo. How can anyone possibly predict the future?

鮑伯，我很驚訝你會相信那玩意。那只不過是一堆胡言亂語罷了。任何人怎麼可能會預知未來？

B: The last time I went to my fortune teller, she warned me not to make any financial adjustments. The next day, the stock I was going to buy fell ten points. ***I could have lost a lot of money if I hadn't gone to her.***

我最後一次去找算命先生時，她警告我不宜做任何財務調動。第二天，我要買的股票就跌了十點。如果我沒去找她，我就會損失一大筆錢。

A: That's just a coincidence. How could she possibly know your stock portfolio?

那只是湊巧罷了。她怎麼可能會知道你的股票呢？

B: I don't know. But that was the third time she was right. I'd rather believe her words.

我不知道。但這是她第三次靈驗了。我是寧可信其有，不可信其無的。

** astrology〔ə'strɑlədʒɪ〕*n.* 占星術　***mumbo jumbo*** 胡言亂語
predict〔prɪ'dɪkt〕*v.* 預知；預測
coincidence〔ko'ɪnsədəns〕*n.* 湊巧
portfolio〔port'folɪ,o〕*n.* 有價證券

Part 8 熱門話題6

視聽中心和卡拉OK

MTV & Karaoke

Music Television

MTV 視聽中心和卡拉OK是台北的兩大流行休閒去處。對於老外而言，這必定是個新鮮的名詞，你可以適時地為他們介紹。

Dialogue:

B: I know that you have been working hard on this for a week now. Why don't you take a rest? ***Get out tonight and kick up your heels a little.*** 我知道你已經忙了一星期了。爲什麼你不休息一下？今晚出去狂歡一下。

A: Wow! thank you, Mr. Chang. But I'm afraid I'm still a bit new in Taiwan. Can you recommend any places to go? 哇！謝謝你，張先生。但是我對台灣不太熟悉。你可否推薦我一些休閒去處？

B: Well, many of the foreigners like to go to the MTV centers to watch movies. 嗯，很多外國人喜歡去MTV視聽中心看影片。

A: I've seen those centers everywhere. What are they? You know, in the States, MTV is a television channel. 我在各地都看到過這些中心。那是什麼？你知道的，在美國MTV是一個電視頻道。

** ***kick up one's heel*** 狂歡　　recommend〔,rɛkə'mɛnd〕*v.* 推薦

B： I knew that. Here, ***it's a video store with a place to watch it***. You get your own private living room to watch a movie. And you get a free coffee or coke with the film.
我知道。在這裡，它是提供房間和錄影帶給人觀賞的地方。你可以獨自在房間裡看影片。並且供應免費的咖啡或可樂。

A：Well, I don't feel like seeing a movie alone.
嗯，我不喜歡獨自一個人看影片。

B： Then ***why don't you join me at the " karaoke "***？
那麼，爲什麼你不和我一起去「卡拉 OK 」呢？

A：What's that？那是什麼？

B： ***It means orchestra without accompaniment***. They play taped music and the customers get up and sing the words. But you can just sit and have a drink if you like. You don't have to sing.
那是一座沒有伴奏的樂隊。他們放出錄音帶，並且讓客人上台去唱歌。但是，如果你喜歡，可以只坐在椅子上喝酒。你不一定要唱歌。

A：***That sounds great***. I can watch you perform.
聽起來不錯。我可以看你表演。

** channel〔'tʃænl̩〕*n*. 頻道　orchestra〔'ɔrkɪstrə〕*n*. 樂隊
accompaniment〔ə'kʌmpənɪmənt〕*n*. 伴奏
perform〔pɚ'fɔrm〕*v*. 表演

Part 4 雜誌閱讀充電指南

在**資訊爆炸**的今天，誰能最快掌握資訊，誰就掌握了成功的先機。因此，工商業人士在繁忙的業務之外，還必須隨時爲自己**充電加油**。無論是加强專業知識或是通曉世界經濟動態，對一個想成功的企業人而言，這更是每天必行的作業。

擷取新知・擴展視野

但這項作業要從何而起呢？除了翻閱留心每日的報紙之外，閱讀國外最具權威性的**雜誌**就是明瞭國際現況的最佳途徑。其中尤以 **TIME**（**時代周刊**）最爲膾炙人口，其知名度與權威性更是無人能出其右。TIME 的內容主體是由許多**專欄**（***sections***）所組成，其中最受工商業界人士歡迎的是***Economy & Business***（**經貿專欄**），其內容層面廣泛，題材多樣化，提供讀者從各種不同角度來觀看世界經貿問題，舉凡全球股市動盪不安，日圓升值等問題，皆有獨到的評論與報告。這些具有前瞻性的文章，更是值得上班族們研讀，進而廣收資訊擷取新知，**擴展視野**以認清國際潮流，才能跟上國際化的脚步，做個**高附加值**的上班族。

掌握必備字彙

但是面對艱澀甚至刁鑽的**生字**，一味地查字典只會減低你的閱讀興趣，因此本章特列出**必備字彙**一單元，將常出現在貿易新聞中的單字列出以幫助你的閱讀。只要你不斷保持閱讀習慣，不假時日，這些世界動態，將是你邁向成功的踏脚石。

在此亦建議你不妨先從較**簡易的雜誌**著手，例如***Newsweek*** 等，以建立信心。這些雜誌的文字不若 TIME 艱深，但內容卻依然具有可讀性；在一段時間後，即可向 TIME 挑戰了。

另外，一些較軟性的雜誌也可以作爲休閒充電之用，這些雜誌的內容通常是包羅萬象，無奇不有。從世界采風錄、流行服飾、藝文小品，到一些道聽塗說的明星軼聞都有。這些生活中的小挿曲，也可以在增進英文閱讀能力之外，爲你的生活加些**色彩**與**創意**。對從事於動腦工作的上班族而言，更可以激發你工作上的創意與思考層面，眞可謂一舉數得，何樂而不爲呢？

現在，你就可以查閱本章的「**國外知名雜誌訂閱辦法**」，看看你對哪一本雜誌最感興趣，馬上就開始爲你的事業和英語能力加油充電吧！

1 國外知名雜誌訂閱辦法

⑴ 向書店零買，但不如訂閱划算。

⑵ 向台灣的**代理公司**訂閱。台灣英文雜誌社即代理「*Newsweek*」、「*U.S. News & World Report*」等雜誌。知名的「*Reader's Digest*」（讀者文摘）在台亦有代理公司。

⑶ 若在台灣無代理公司，則必需向當地的雜誌社，或透過**香港、日本**的分公司訂購。通常可先在書報攤上購得零售本，再將內附的「**訂閱單**」（*order sheet*），填好寄出，並寄上訂費，即可。若無法在坊間書報攤買到零售本，則可直接寫信到雜誌社，索取「訂閱單」。一般的雜誌社會設有一段收到新書的期限，若在期限內，尚未收到新書，可以郵件向對方連繫。

2 國外知名雜誌訂閱地址費用

· **THE NEW YOKER**
（紐約客）
《訂費》one year U.S. $ 56.00
payable in advance
《地址》Box 56447, Boulder,
Colorado 80322

· **TIME**（時代週刊）
《訂費》one year NT $ 2,964
《地址》TIME international Inc.
(Taiwan Branch), Fl.
9 No. 24 Section 1, Nan
King Eastern Road, 10407
Taipei, Taiwan, R.O.C.
北市南京東路一段24號9樓

· **NEWSWEEK**（新聞週刊）
《訂費》30 weeks NT$1,440
52 weeks NT$2,340
78 weeks NT$3,120
104 weeks NT$4,160
《地址》台北郵政信箱65號
總代理：台灣英文雜誌社有限公司

· **READER'S DIGEST**
（讀者文摘）
《訂費》one year NT $ 1080.00
《地址》Reader's Digest (East
Asia) Ltd. P.O. Box
56-7, Taipei

· **NATIONAL GEOGRAPHIC**
（國家地理雜誌）
《訂費》15-month U.S. $ 32.50
《地址》Post Office Box 2895
Washington, D.C. 20077-9960

· **SEVENTEEN**（十七歲）
《訂費》one year U.S. $ 27.00
《地址》Radnor, Pennsylvania 19088

· **VOGUE**（時尚）
《訂費》one year U.S. $ 49
payable in advance
《地址》Vogue, Box 5201, Boulder,
Co. 80322

· **U.S. News & World Report**
（美國新聞與世界報導）
《訂費》one year U.S. $ 39.75
《地址》台北郵政信箱65號
總代理：台灣英文雜誌社有限公司

· **FORTUNE INTERNATIONAL**
（財星）
《訂費》one year NT $ 2,600
《地址》Taishih Magazine Co. Ltd.
2E, Cathay Alexandre
Mansion 9 Lane, 464 Tun
Hwa S. Road Taipei, 106
Taiwan R.O.C.

3 1990全球十大要聞

■ **IRAQ INVADES KUWAIT**, making hostages of thousands of foreigners and setting off a worldwide military response.
伊拉克入侵科威特，扣留數千名外國人質，並造成全球武裝反應。

* GULF CRISIS—The U.N. Security Council authorized a U.S.-led force to drive Iraq from Kuwait, five months after Saddam Hussein seized the emirate.
波斯灣危機—在海珊入侵科威特後五個月，聯合國安理會授權一支以美國爲主導的武力，將伊拉克逐出科威特。

■ **EAST AND WEST GERMANY REUNITE** after more than four decades as separate countries.
在分隔了八十年之後的東西德終於統一。

* A whirlwind year of historic change culminated Oct. 3 in unification, following Moscow's approval of German membership in NATO.
在莫斯科方面同意德國加入北大西洋公約組織後，這旋風式歷史性變化的一年，在十月三日達到統一的最高潮。。

■ **POLITICAL AND ECONOMIC REFORMS** throw Soviet Union into turmoil; moves toward sovereignty are afoot in all 15 republics.
政經改革使蘇聯陷入一片混亂，朝向主權獨立的行動正在十五個共和國中展開。

■ **BUDGET DEBATE** between Congress and president drags on for five months before package containing tax increases is approved.

美總統和國會雙方就預算案激辯了五個月，才使關於增稅的法案通過。

■ **U.S. ECONOMY SUFFERS A SLUMP**; layoffs and foreclosures rise throughout the country.

美國經濟不景氣，全國正彌漫一股裁員及取消贖回抵押權之風。

■ **FLEDGLING DEMOCRACIES IN EASTERN EUROPE** are threatened by ethnic turmoil, economic hardship.

東歐新民主政體正飽受民族紛爭及經濟頓困的威脅。

* Elation over the toppling of Nicolae Ceausescu's dictatorial regime was quickly replaced by bickering that frequently spilled over into street violence.

推翻尼古拉・西奧塞古獨裁政權之後的歡騰，已迅速地被頻繁的街頭暴力所產生的動盪不安所取代。

■ **PANAMANIAN PRESIDENT MANUEL NORIEGA SURRENDERS** and is brought to the United States to stand trial on charges of accepting bribes from drug traffickers.

巴拿馬軍事强人諾利加投降，並被送往美國受審，他被控接受毒梟的賄賂。

* Manuel Noriega surrendered to U.S. forces on Jan. 3, and the country began to rebuild from the devastation of the American invasion.

* In a historic year, the Communist Party lost its constitutionally guaranteed monopoly on political power and Gorbachev survived a revolt by the republics and a challenge from Boris Yeltsin and opponents to his plans for the switch to a market economy.

在歷史性的一年中，共黨失去了在政治上長久以來所把持專制政體，而戈巴契夫則深受共和國內的叛變及來自葉爾欽及反對其市場經濟計畫人士的挑戰。

■ **THE U.S. SAVINGS-AND-LOAN BAILOUT** grows larger, touching the president's son and five senators.

美國政府對銀行界的融資救濟金額日益龐大，並使總統的兒子及五位參議員涉案。

■ **RELATIONS WARM** between the United States and Soviet Union. 美蘇關係日趨緩和。

一月三日諾利加向美軍軀服；自此這個國家開始在美國入侵後的殘破中重建家園。

■ **BRITISH PRIME MINISTER MARGARET THATCHER** steps down.
英首相柴契爾夫人下台。

* John Major, the 47-year-old treasury chief who left school at 16, took over as prime minister Nov. 28 after a Conservative Party rebellion against Mrs. Thatcher.
十六歲即輟學的四十七歲財政首長，約翰・梅傑，十一月二十八日在保守黨對柴契爾夫人提出不信任之後，接下首相的職位。

4 看懂商業新聞必備單字

A

- acquisition〔ˌækwəˈzɪʃən〕*n.* 企業吞併
- administration〔ədˌmɪnəˈstreʃən〕*n.* 經營；管理
- analyst〔ˈænəlɪst〕*n.* 分析家
- ***announcement***〔əˈnaʊnsmənt〕*n.* 通知；發表
- attest〔əˈtɛst〕*v.* 證實；證明
- alliance〔əˈlaɪəns〕*n.* 同盟關係　asset〔ˈæsɛts〕*n.pl.* 資產

B

- balance〔ˈbæləns〕*n.* 差額；平衡
- blockbuster〔ˈblɑkˌbʌstɚ〕*n.* 非常成功之作
- bond〔bɑnd〕*n.* 債券；契約　***boom***〔bum〕*n.* 景氣；突趨繁榮
- budget〔ˈbʌdʒɪt〕*n.* 預算

C

- capitalism〔ˈkæpətl̩ˌɪzəm〕*n.* 資本主義
- ***Capitol Hill*** 國會山莊
- ***circulation***〔ˌsɝkjəˈleʃən〕*n.* 貨幣的流通
- concede〔kənˈsid〕*v.* 讓與；忍讓　congress〔ˈkɑŋgrəs〕*n.* 國會
- corporate〔ˈkɔrpərɪt〕*adj.* 法人的
- crash〔kræʃ〕*n.*（股市）崩潰

D

· debt〔 dɛt 〕*n*. 借款；債務　decade〔 'dɛked 〕*n*. 十年

· decline〔 dɪ'klaɪn 〕*v*. 下降；下跌　***deficit***〔 'dɛfəsɪt 〕*n*. 赤字

· ***deflation***〔 dɪ'fleʃən 〕*n*. 通貨緊縮

· discipline〔 'dɪsəplɪn 〕*n*. 訓練；鍛鍊

· depression〔 dɪ'prɛʃən 〕*n*. 不景氣；蕭條

E

· ***economic***〔 ,ikə'nɑmɪk 〕*adj*. 經濟的

· elaborate〔 ɪ'læbərɪt 〕*adj*. 講究的

· ***eliminate***〔 ɪ'lɪmə,net 〕*v*. 淘汰

· exchange〔 ɪks'tʃendʒ 〕*v*. 兌換；交換；交易

· executive〔 ɪg'zɛkjʊtɪv 〕*adj*. 行政的

· expand〔 ɪk'spænd 〕*v*. 擴展　external〔 ɪk'stɝnḷ 〕*adj*. 對外的

F

· facilitate〔 fə'sɪlə,tet 〕*v*. 使便利

· federal〔 'fɛdərəl 〕*adj*. 聯邦的　feign〔 fen 〕*v*. 假裝

· finance〔 fə'næns , 'faɪnæns 〕*n*. 財政

· ***fiscal***〔 'fɪskḷ 〕*adj*. 國庫的；會計的

· friction〔 'frɪkʃən 〕*n*. 摩擦；衝突　***fuel***〔 'fjuəl 〕*n*. 燃料

G

· GATT 關稅貿易一般協定（＝*General Agreement on Tariffs and Trade*）　globe〔 glob 〕*n*. 全球

· GNP 國民生產毛額（＝*Gross National Product*）

· grasp〔græsp〕*v*. 抓住；握緊
· gratis〔'gretɪs, 'grætɪs〕*adj*. 免費的
· guile〔gaɪl〕*n*. 欺詐；狡猾　***guild***〔gɪld〕*n*. 同業公會

H

· halt〔hɔlt〕*v*. 阻止　hawk〔hɔk〕*v*. 散播；叫賣
· heckle〔'hɛkḷ〕*v*. 激烈質問　heed〔hid〕*n*. 注意；留心
· herald〔'hɛrəld〕*n*. 發佈人
· ***heritage***〔'hɛrətɪdʒ〕*n*. 祖產

I

· implement〔'ɪmplə,mɛnt〕*v*. 實現
· inflation〔ɪn'fleʃən〕*n*. 通貨膨脹
· ***innovation***〔,ɪnə'veʃən〕*n*. 革新
· inquiry〔ɪn'kwaɪrɪ, 'ɪnkwərɪ〕*n*. 調查；質問
· interest〔'ɪntərɪst〕*n*. 利息
· investment〔ɪn'vɛstmənt〕*n*. 投資

J

· judicial〔dʒu'dɪʃəl〕*adj*. 司法的　juggle〔'dʒʌgḷ〕*v*. 做假
· ***junction***〔'dʒʌŋkʃən〕*n*. 聯絡

K

· keen〔kin〕*adj*. 銳利的；鋒利的　knock〔nɑk〕*v*. 敲打
· knowledge〔'nɑlɪdʒ〕*n*. 情報；見聞
· ***Kremlin***〔'krɛmlɪm〕*n*. 克里姆林宮

L

- lacerate〔'læsə,ret〕*v*. 撕裂　laconic〔lə'kɑnɪk〕*adj*. 簡潔的
- lag〔læg〕*v*. 落後；延遲　***ledger***〔'lɛdʒɚ〕*n*. 總帳
- leech〔litʃ〕*n*. 高利貸　local〔'lokḷ〕*adj*. 本地的

M

- manipulate〔mə'nɪpjə,let〕*v*. 操縱
- marginal〔'mɑrdʒɪnḷ〕*adj*. 最低的
- ***materialism***〔mə'tɪrɪə,lɪzṃ〕*n*. 唯物論；物質主義
- merge〔'mɝdʒ〕*v*. 合併　migrate〔'maɪgret〕*v*. 移居；移動
- modulus〔'mɑdʒələs〕*n*. 係數　***monopoly***〔mə'nɑpḷɪ〕*n*. 壟斷

N

- naught〔nɔt〕*n*. 零　***neutralize***〔'njutrə,laɪz〕*v*. 使無效
- nexus〔'nɛksəs〕*n*. 連結　nominate〔'nɑmə,net〕*v*. 任命
- ***numerical***〔nju'mɛrɪkḷ〕*adj*. 數的；數字上的

O

- obtain〔əb'ten〕*v*. 獲得　***operate***〔'ɑpə,ret〕*v*. 工作；運轉
- outlay〔'aʊt,le〕*n*. 開銷　opposite〔'ɑpəzɪt〕*adj*. 相反的

P

- plunge〔plʌndʒ〕*v*. 陷落；跳入
- ***profit***〔'prɑfɪt〕*n*. 利潤；盈餘　propose〔prə'poz〕*v*. 提議
- ***prosperity***〔prɑs'pɛrətɪ〕*n*. 繁榮
- pressure〔'prɛʃɚ〕*n*. 壓力；壓迫

Q

- quadruple〔'kwɑdrupl̩〕*adj*. 四倍的
- qualify〔'kwɑlə,faɪ〕*v*. 使有資格　quality〔'kwɑlətɪ〕*n*. 品質
- quantity〔'kwɑntətɪ〕*n*. 量　***quota***〔'kwotə〕*n*. 分配

R

- rally〔'rælɪ〕*v*. 召集；(景氣)恢復　ratio〔'reʃo〕*n*. 比例
- ***recession***〔rɪ'sɛʃən〕*n*. 蕭條　release〔rɪ'lis〕*v*. 發表
- rescind〔rɪ'sɪnd〕*v*. 宣告(法律、條約)無效
- ***revenue***〔'rɛvə,nju〕*n*. 歲入　reserve〔rɪ'zɝv〕*v*. 預訂

S

- setback〔'sɛt,bæk〕*n*. 敗北；妨礙
- sluggish〔'slʌgɪʃ〕*adj*. 不景氣的；緩慢的
- ***slump***〔slʌmp〕*n*. 暴跌　speculate〔'spɛkjə,let〕*v*. 投機
- statistics〔stə'tɪstɪks〕*n*. 統計　stock〔stɑk〕*n*. 股票
- strategy〔'strætədʒɪ〕*n*. 戰略；策略
- ***surplus***〔'sɝplʌs〕*n*. 盈餘

T

- tariff〔'tærɪf〕*n*. 關稅
- technology〔tɛk'nɑlədʒɪ〕*n*. 科技
- toll〔tol〕*n*. 代價；費用　trauma〔'traʊmə〕*n*. 傷害
- ***trigger***〔'trɪgɚ〕*n*. 誘因　troop〔trup〕*n*. 軍隊

U

· unanimous〔 jʊ'nænəməs 〕*adj*. 同意的；一致同意的
· undergo〔 ,ʌndɚ'go 〕*v*. 經過；遭受
· ***undertake***〔 ,ʌndɚ'tek 〕*v*. 承辦；擔任
· ultimate〔 'ʌltəmɪt 〕*adj*. 最終的　　ultra〔 'ʌltrə 〕*adj*. 極端的
· utility〔 ju'tɪlətɪ 〕*n*. 實用；效用

V

· vacant〔 'vekənt 〕*adj*. 空缺的
· vacillate〔 'væsə,let 〕*v*. 搖動；擺動
· ***valuation***〔 ,væljʊ'eʃən 〕*n*. 評價
· vast〔 væst 〕*adj*. 巨大的；巨額的
· venality〔 vi'nælətɪ 〕*n*. 貪污
· ***venture***〔 'vɛntʃɚ 〕*n*. 冒險；投機　　void〔 vɔɪd 〕*adj*. 無效的

W

· wealth〔 wɛlθ 〕*n*. 財富；財產　　whirl〔 hwɝl 〕*v*. 使旋轉
· wholesaler〔 'hol,selɚ 〕*n*. 批發業者

Y

· yield〔 jild 〕*v*. 出產　　Yen〔 jɛn 〕*n*. 日圓

Z

· zealot〔 'zɛlət 〕*n*. 狂熱份子
· zone〔 zon 〕*n*. 地區

5 國內知名雜誌英文名稱

□ 天下雜誌	Commonwealth
□ 卓越	Excellence
□ 管理雜誌	Management Magazine
□ 商業週刊	Business Weekly
□ 大都會	Metropolitan
□ 財星週刊	Fortune Weekly
□ 新新聞	The Journalist
□ 遠見	Global Views Monthly
□ 錢	Money
□ 講義	Better Life Monthly
□ 婦女雜誌	The Woman
□ 休閒	Leisure Life Monthly
□ 號外	City Magazine
□ 統領	Leader
□ 直效行銷	Direct Selling & Marketing Magazine
□ 住宅情報	Housing Information
□ 拾穗	Gleaners
□ 中國男人	The Man Magazine
□ 周末	Weekend
□ 時報周刊	China Times Weekly
□ 聯合文學	Unitas

●在下列各書局可以買到學習出版公司之書籍及錄音帶

●台北市●
重南書局
文翔書局
眾文書局
永大書局
巨擘書局
新智書局
正文書局
弘雅書局
文友書局
博大書局
致遠書局
千華書局
曉園書局
建宏書局
宏業書局
文康書局
光統書局
文源書局
翰輝書局
文化書局
正元書局
天龍書局
金石堂
文化廣場
建德書報社
貞德書報社
百全書報社
聯宏書報社
聯豐書報社
華一書報社
偉正書報社
恒立書報社
中台書報社
建興書局
文笙書局
大中國書局
國聯書局
宏一書局
宏昇書局
百文書局
鴻儒堂書局
廣城書局
學語書局
南陽書局
三友書局
華星書局
新學友書局
來來百貨
永漢書局
力行書局
泰堂書局
金橋圖書股
份有限公司
文普書局
力霸百貨
集太祥書局
偉群書局
萬泰書局
明志書局
宏玉書局
興來百貨
文佳書局
自力書局
誼美書局
水準書局
中美書局
頂淵書局
今日書局
長樂書局
德昌書局
敦煌書局
松芳書局
弘文書局
統領書局
啓文書局
永琦書局
鴻源百貨
敬恒書局
新光百貨
益群書局
聯一書局
朝陽堂
六福堂書局
博文堂書局
益民書局
捨而美書局
百葉書局
今博書局
鑫日書局
太華書局
平峰書局
百合書局
朝陽書局
天才學局
久大書
香世界
東利書局
聯合資訊
天下電腦
信宏書局
校園書局
中興大學
圖書部
合歡書局
博聞堂書局
政大書局
再興書局
建安書局
文理書局
華一書局
伯樂書局
東光百
貨公司
宏明書局
建國書局
中建書局
師大書局
浦公英書局
夢溪書局
時報出版社
宏欣書局
桂冠出版社
九章出版社
開發書局
智邦書局
永豐餘
永星書局
漢昇書局
慈暉書局
達仁書局
新興書局
明志工專
崇文圖書
廣奧書局
進文堂書局
福勝書局
台大書局
書林書局
景儷書局
香草山書局
漢記書局
光啓書局
增文堂書局
富美書局
益中書局
葉山書局
漢文書局
師大書苑
學海書局
克明書局
華城書局
崇暉書局
來來書局
青草地書局
實踐書坊
人人書局
文軒書局
升華書局
大學書局
東成書局
長青書局
玉山書局
亨得利書局
文達書局
光華書局
冠德書局
宗記書局
士林書局
宇文書局
擰檬黃書局
大漢書局
信加書局
勝一書局
兒童百科
書局

●永和●
東豐書局
國中書局
宇城書局
潮流書局
文德書局
大方書局
超群書局
文山書局
三通書局

●中和●
景新書局
華陽書局

●新店●
華泰書局
文風書局
勝博書局
文山書局
宏德書局

●板橋●
永一書局
優豪電腦
建盈書局
賢明書局
流行站百貨
恒隆書局
啓文書局
峰國書局
文林書局
文人書局
文城書局
大漢書局
大有爲書局

●三重●
義記書局
日新書局
文海書局
百勝書局
仁人書局

●新莊●
珠海書局
鴻陽書局
文林書局
辰陽書局
崇文圖書

●泰山鄉●
大雅書局

●淡水●
文理書局
匯林書局
淡友書局
國寶書局
匯文書局
中外書局

●羅東●
翰林書局
統一書局
學人書局
三民學局
國泰書局
環華書局
國民書局

●宜蘭●
華山書局
金隆書局
新時代書局
四季風書局
方向書局

●花蓮●
千歲書坊
中原書局
新生書局
精藝書坊

●台東●
徐氏書局
統一書局

●金門●
翰林書局
源成書局
金鴻福書局

●澎湖●
大眾書局
黎明書局

●桃園●
文化書局
中山書局
天寧書局
東方書局

東海書局
大新書局
奇奇書局
全國優良圖
書展藍源德
好學生書局

●中壢●

立德書局
文明書局
文化書局
貞德書局
建宏書局
博士書局
奇奇書局
大學書局

●新竹●

大學書局
昇大書局
六藝出版社
竹一書局
仁文書局
學府書局
文華書局
黎明書局
文國書局
金鼎獎書局
大新書局
文山書局
弘文書局
德興書局
學風書局
泰昌書局
滋朗書局
排行榜書局
光南書局
大華書報社

●苗栗●

益文書局
芙華書局
建國書局
文華書局

●基隆●

文粹書局
育德書局
自立書局
明德書局
中興書局
文隆書局
建國書局
文豐書局

●台中市●

宏明書局
曉園出版社
台中門市
滄海書局
大學圖書
供應社
逢甲書局
聯經出版社
中央書局
大衆書局
新大方書局
中華書局
文軒書局
柏林書局
亞勝補習班
文化書城
三民書局
台一書局
興大書局
興大書齋
興大文書局
正文書局
新能書局
新學友學局
全文書局
國鼎書局
國賓書局
華文書局
建國書局
汗牛書屋
享聲唱片行
華中書局
逢甲大學
諾貝爾書局
中部書報社
中一書局
明道書局
振文書局
中台一專
盛文書局

●台中縣●

三民書局
建成書局
欣欣唱片行
大千書局
中一書局
明道書局

●彰化●

復文書局
東門書局
新新書局
台聯書局
時代書局
成功書局
世界書局
來來書局
翰林書局
一新書局
中山書局
文明書局

●雲林●

建中書局
大山書局
文芳書局
國光書局
良昌書局
三民書局

●嘉義市●

文豐書局
慶隆盛書局
義豐書局
志成書局
大漢書局
書苑庭書局
學英公司
天才書局
學英書局
光南書局
嘉聯書報社

●嘉義縣●

建成書局

●台南縣●

全勝書局
博大書局
第一書局
南一書局
柳營書局

●台南市●

欣欣文化社
光南唱片行
嘉南書社
第一書局
東華書局
成功大學
書局部
成大書城
文山書局
孟子書局
大友書局
松文書局
盛文書局
台南書局
日勝書局
旭日書局
南台圖書
公司
金寶書局
船塢書坊
南一書局
大統唱片行
國正書局
源文書局
永茂書報社
天才書局

●高雄縣●

延平書局
欣良書局
大岡山書城
時代書局
鳳山大書城
遠東大書城
天下書局
杏綱書局
統一書局
百科書局
志成書局
光遠書局

●高雄市●

高雄書報社
宏昇書局
理想書局
高文堂書局
松柏書局
三民書局
光南書局
國鼎書局
文英書局
黎明書局
光明書局
前程書局
[illegible]行書局
登文書局
青山外語
補習班
六合書局
美新書局
朝代書局
意文書局
地下街
文化廣場
大立百貨公
司圖書部
大統百貨公
司圖書部
黎明文化
有前書局
建工書局
鐘樓書局
青年書局
瓊林書局
大學城書局
引想力書局
永大書局
杏莊書局
儒林書局
雄大書局
復文書局
致遠書局
明仁書局
宏亞書局
瀚文書局
天祥書局
廣文書局
楊氏書局
慈珊書局
盛文書局
光統
圖書百貨
愛偉書局

●屏東●

復文書局
建利書局
百成書局
新星書局
百科書局
屏東書城
屏東唱片行
英格文教社
賢明書局
大古今書局
屏東農專
圖書部
順時書局
百順書局

心得筆記欄

上班族充電英語

編　　著／陳 怡 平
發 行 所／學習出版有限公司　☎ (02) 2704-5525
郵撥帳號／0512727-2 學習出版社帳戶
登 記 證／局版台業 2179 號
印 刷 所／裕強彩色印刷有限公司
台北門市／臺北市許昌街 10 號 2 F　☎ (02) 2331-4060·2331-9209
台中門市／台中市綠川東街 32 號 8 F 23 室　☎ (04) 223-2838
台灣總經銷／紅螞蟻圖書有限公司　☎ (02) 2799-9490·2657-0132
美國總經銷／Evergreen Book Store　☎ (818) 2813622

售價：新台幣二百二十元正

2000 年 9 月 1 日一版五刷

ISBN 957-519-298-2